Contents

Foreword

The problems facing a Social Services Department because of the daunting demographic trends of greatly increased numbers of elderly people in the population are very real ones for East Sussex. One in ten of our population is over the age of 75 which is double the national average.

As soon as we reasonably could after the Seebohm reorganisation therefore we embarked on a research programme to see how we could wisely and more effectively use our budget for services for elderly people. We followed this with the development of policies and priorities in working with elderly people leading to the adoption by Social Services Committee of a Statement of Objectives.

An important part of this process was the need to look hard at how we care for our elderly people and how we promote self-care. We were most fortunate that the Department of Health and Social Security Social Work Service Development Group with its considerable expertise were prepared to accept my invitation to help us to do this. What is more they 'stayed with us' after the hard work to help implement some of the changes we wished to make as a result of our joint work.

The programme had to be undertaken in one Division so as not to diffuse it and Brighton rose to the challenge. It opened our eyes to our faults and weaknesses but it was also a very positive experience. It gave staff a tremendous fillip and enabled many of them to move forward more quickly, more effectively and with much more confidence into change. Its message has reverberated across the County and inspired many developments and experiments in less traditional ways of working with and caring for elderly people.

I know staff would wish to join with me in thanking the Development Group for working with us on this project and I hope this volume will encourage others working with elderly people.

Denis Allen
Director of Social Services
EAST SUSSEX

February 1980

Preface

This is the report of a development project carried out in one division of East Sussex Social Services Department. It focussed on the services provided for elderly people in Brighton in the light of their increasing numbers and increasing frailty. The Development Group, in mounting the project, does not claim to have discovered anything new – most of the ideas which were discussed and promulgated have been about for a good many years – but its aims were to re-examine with those most closely involved what was happening in this field of work in Brighton, and to help them bring about changes which would benefit the elderly clients. It was hoped that the project itself and the changes it brought about would have wider repercussions in the whole field of work with the elderly.

Following the initiative provided by Denis Allen, Director of Social Services for East Sussex and Barbara Kahan, Assistant Director, Social Work Service, many people shared in the project described in this report. The bulk of the work was undertaken by Malcolm Jordan of the Development Group, in conjunction with Pamela Emy of Southern Region SWS.

The project was encouraged throughout by Denis Allen and by Peter Atkins, Divisional Director of Social Services for Brighton, who inspired their staff to work hard in introducing new ways of working and in breaking down entrenched attitudes.

We are grateful to the divisional social services staff in Brighton and those working in homes for the elderly whose papers have been used in the report.

Most of all we should like to thank the elderly people themselves, some of whose pictures appear in the report, who took a great interest in the changes which occurred and without whom the report would not have been written. They have taken an interest in the production of the report, but in order to respect their privacy the names of the residential homes have been changed.

The prime editorial task fell to Pat Corby, who worked on earlier papers produced by Lillien Points. Final editing was carried out by Joan Thurman.

The views expressed in this volume are not intended to represent the policies of the Department of Health & Social Security nor East Sussex Social Services Department.

J Hodder
Principal Social Work Service Officer
SWS DEVELOPMENT GROUP

February 1980

Introduction

Confronted by the daunting demographic trends which, here as in many other countries, describe a situation where the aged within the population will greatly increase in numbers over the next few decades, authorities in many areas have recently been considering how they might attempt to provide for the care and well being of the increasing number of elderly people local communities will be called upon to sustain.

The elderly are not a favoured group for the caring professions. A recent report[1] has thrown into relief the fact that social workers tend to be bored by or indifferent to the problems of those clients who are approaching the final decades of their life. There is little enthusiasm for giving the elderly other than low priority within most workers' caseloads.

Old age and declining powers are predicaments many people will have to face. The common reluctance to bring a total commitment of intellect and imagination to the care of the elderly is perhaps connected with this. People generally fear to look in a mirror which shows their probable decline and decay, and are uneasy at the thought of taking responsibility for parents who have for so long been their models and mentors.

East Sussex Social Services Department was, however, prepared to look at the problem of its increasingly ageing population. The Department asked the Development Group of DHSS Social Work Service to help by mounting a three year project to enquire into patterns of care for the elderly, and its Brighton Division became the focus of the exercise.

The project began with some interviews and studies of elderly people in January 1977. The first 3-day seminar was held in April 1977. This was followed by three working groups which reported in the autumn of 1977. A 2-day seminar was held in February 1978, and further developments followed during this year. A final day seminar was held in March 1979.

This volume is not, in the conventional sense, a report on the experiences of these three years. Readers can find this information elsewhere[2]. Here there is no time sequence of events following one after the other, no faithful reporting of exactly what happened or was said by the various participants. Rather it aims to tell the story of those years and, by giving a bird's eye view of some of the happenings and thinking which arose during the course of the project, to convey something of what the experience meant to those who participated.

Brighton's experience in this matter was of a particular nature. None the less the work carried out in examining how to provide assistance for elderly people, as well as in pondering ways in which it might be improved, has general relevance and may, perhaps, provide a stimulus to the thinking of others endeavouring to move away from the more traditional patterns of care for the elderly.

To the Development Group the project was rather like having an allotment down at Brighton. They went down regularly to help the locals cultivate the plot, husband ideas and promote experiment. The chapters which follow are a distillation of their joint experience. It is not easy to describe what was constantly evolving but they have tried to maintain some balance; between the views of the elderly themselves and those of the workers who care for them; between the developments as they took place and the outcome of all the work. Inevitably some will feel important aspects of the events at Brighton have been neglected. What follows is a selective summary of the total story.

References

[1]*Social Service Teams: The Practitioner's View* Parsloe P, Stevenson O. DHSS Report Published HMSO. 1978

[2]*Patterns of Care for the Elderly.* Parts I, II and III and short summary of developments, March 1979 available on request from the Development Group, DHSS, Alexander Fleming House, Elephant and Castle, London SE1 6BY

‘I don’t mind being on my own at all, but on the other hand you have to have a little bit of company haven’t you?’

Some elderly people in Brighton – their views

It seems right to begin this volume with the view of elderly people themselves – because all else flows from this point.

The Project Planning Group was anxious to gain first-hand information from elderly people in the hope that this might form a solid base for the work to come. In initiating a series of interviews with them it was expected that, from the outset, the project would be firmly grounded in the day to day experiences of the people who mattered, the recipients of the service provided by the Brighton Division of East Sussex Social Services Department.

Fifteen people were interviewed in their own homes and others in residential care. The ages of those interviewed ranged from 62 to 93. The average age of those interviewed in their own homes was 83 years. Average ages of the residents are given in Table 1 on page 50. All the interviews were tape recorded and what follows are extracts from the recorded material. A description of the method employed in collecting the material along with fuller details of the interviews can be read elsewhere[1].

The first part of this chapter deals with people in their own homes, some of whom were contemplating admission to residential care. The feelings of the group of residents come next, about the loss of their homes, followed by a description of what they felt about their daily experiences once they became residents. A few comments from interviewees about their rights and status lead into a report of the first Residents' Conference held in Brighton, where residents' rights were a major focus for discussion.

Staying in the community

Being cut off and isolated Many elderly people have a pervading sense of being alone, cut off from their remaining friends and family as well as from the mainstream of living which passes them by. This is what was found in Brighton.

A number of things made it difficult for the elderly people to gain any feeling of belonging to the community at large. Many lived in rented or owner-occupied accommodation on run-down estates. The other householders were often young married couples – and many were out at work as well as being preoccupied with the task of bringing up children. Where neighbours were older they tended to be incapacitated in some way, either by age or physical handicap, and they too were unable to move out of their home and visit others.

The daytime was the worst time for them. Panic can soon take over when there is no one active enough to help within hailing distance.

'All the old ones have died out, no one now, they have all faded out, there's no one to come visiting, they used to when I first come years ago they used to come and see me, plenty of able bodied ones, like to come and have a chat and a cuppa tea but now there doesn't seem to be anyone'.

'Well, I'm nervous because of falling. I've had two falls fairly recently and it's such a job to get up, I can't go on my knees because they are all out of shape. Yes it's a terrible job to get up, and I get nervous now in case I fall and there is nobody there to help me. There is a young couple live opposite who never come near me, they have not spoken to me for months, they never come near, never do anything for me, they never enquire whether I'm dead or alive so I can't rely on them'.

'I hadn't got the tablets and I've been in pain and nobody's been in for about five days and he came, gave me the prescription, well I'd got no one to get it for me, and I kept calling next door. I thought if I can make them hear they will go, and I waited till 5 o'clock and then I started to call and I was calling her till 5.50 and I couldn't make them hear. And then by all accounts, I don't know, apparently one of them came into the back door and I was shouting for my daughter who was dead so I'd got hysterical. I'm so alone I've got no one. I kind of feel now that I'm being boxed in. Can you understand what I mean?'

'I've got one or two friends around here, for instance, a lady looks in – she is a married lady and has three children, I've known her for a very long time and she comes along here on Friday afternoon to do shopping, and she will call around and we will have a cup of tea together which is very nice. I enjoy it very much. She talks about her family and I tell her about mine. We have nice little chats together and I think if some of the old people would like some of the visitors to go, just have a cup of tea or a little chat for a short time it would take some of the loneliness off. I'm very fond of TV,

I turn that on, I have the radio. I don't mind being on my own at all, but on the other hand you have to have a little bit of company haven't you?'

Visits from outside the immediate estate were not easy to come by either. Relatives and friends were themselves older and less mobile. Public transport was infrequent and, for pensioners, extremely expensive. Those with cars did not necessarily think of using them to take an elderly person out 'for a little trip'.

'Yes, transport, a very big problem 'cos it would be nice if now and again *now and again mind you*, in the summer somebody could come and just give you a little car drive, not caravans, just a little car ride, take you for a little blow somewhere and bring you back again. It would be a nice little break for you. Because you see I'm not able, it's those steps I can't get down, my son would take me but I can't get down and he cannot lift me down, so I have as much air as I can with the back door, the front door open'.

The telephone A telephone can be a lifeline and reduce isolation. Seven of those interviewed had telephones (four of them through social services) and this provided the owners with some sense of security. Often there was a daily phone call from a neighbour or relative and help could be summoned in an emergency.

'You see for instance, last Thursday my son, phoned. I had the phone which is very useful and I think all old people should have the phone'.

Official visitors and support in living at home Monotony was sometimes interrupted by an official visitor. However, the elderly people interviewed were often confused as to whether the caller was a social worker, health visitor or volunteer. Visits by social workers were, on the whole, appreciated. They were, however, infrequent and often very brief.

'A nice little lady, can't remember her name, they're all so busy that we can't expect too much'.

'The only visitor I get is once every couple of months a young lady comes up here and says, "Good morning Mr Elder, how are you?" and thank you very much, well how am I? I can't tell. I may have an off day, and I may feel quite fit. Well, just now I am fit, I get very bad headaches sometimes, dizziness which is hardening of the arteries as the doctor puts it. That would be all right for me, I'm not very difficult to please, I mean I don't want the world, if you can understand me. All I want is to be able just to go about, mind my own business, but always have somebody watching to see if I am OK. I have got a fear of collapsing again like I did in the road. I haven't really got over that; it was a shock 'cos I don't know what happened, how it happened, I simply know that they picked me up and put me at the side of the road and sat me down. I came round and they brought me home, but it made me nervous, made me very nervous. All I know is about an occasional visitor about once every two months'.

General practitioners were, on the whole, welcome visitors and, for some of the group, visits by them were a regular occurrence. The other regular official visitor for eight clients was the nurse – usually to do a dressing of some sort or for bathing. None of those interviewed anticipated that their own GP or nurse would continue to visit and show concern for them should they be admitted to residential care.

The main forms of support in the home received by the group of fifteen clients were home help, meals on wheels and visits from a nurse. Whilst the provision of these services often meant the difference between admission to residential care and continuing life in the community there were problems. The cost was very high and the visits of the home help sometimes so brief (one hour) as to be of doubtful use. Help was rarely thought to be sufficient and many felt that a little more might prevent their having to give up their independent living.

Only seven clients had meals on wheels on a regular basis, and they appreciated this service. Although the delivery of the meals was quick it afforded a brief human contact.

'If I could have somebody come in every day I could be all right here. It's in the morning when I try to get things done. If I can have somebody come in every morning just for an hour and do the necessaries every day I should be all right'.

'I think there are a lot of people about here in Brighton or anywhere that just need somebody to come in and cook the dinner for them, now I can do that myself, I can make myself a cup of tea or cup of coffee or anything I wish and fill my bottle, well anybody to go in and just do a little. That's the thing that's needed. Mind you our dinners are very good, two very good dinners we get'.

(Blind client) 'Anyway last Christmas they said there was going to be nobody in the house and people will not be bothered with me at Christmas; they think I shall want some nursing but I don't. I thought I'd go to one of the homes. I thought I'd go there for a fortnight. It was very nice for me also, but the doctor wants me to go into one of these homes, but I don't want to at present. I want to keep on this little home as long as I can. If I have a home help every day and cooks me a bit of food and keeps my clothes tidy I am quite satisfied'.

'Well, you see, you do little things for yourself and it helps you a bit more. You get the nurse once a week but you have got to keep yourself clean the rest of the week haven't you? I am very fussy over that, I do try if I could, I would try very hard because I mean I am used to it. But if so being that you could not do it well, there you are, that is the point'.

Clubs Not many wanted to relieve their isolation by belonging to a club for the elderly or handicapped. However, the few who did so enjoyed attending.

'I used to belong to an old folks' club which was run or was supposed to be run by the Lady Mayoress. It was a very nice club, it was in a very nice building, it was very convenient and I used to go every morning regularly for coffee and a game of snooker. Now due to what I considered very bad management or lack of interest, no one cared a damn about the place. It was shut up about eighteen months to two years ago. I never heard anything about it since then. Of course that coincided with the time that I was ill, not well enough to take any interest. But when I did really come round and I wanted to take an interest I found it was closed. Now, to be honest, it was a very good building for a club to be made into a wonderfully convenient and really social club but nobody cares a damn about it. It's just simply left there closed. I don't belong to anything else. I only found out two days ago and there's an old folks' meeting place just along the road here. I haven't been there yet, I don't know anything about it, never see anyone. No one ever mentioned a club again, the only people that I meet is my next door neighbour, a little old lady who is eighty-eight tomorrow or Sunday'.

'I couldn't attempt to go to any clubs. I've lost the use of my legs by keeping indoors, enforced inactivity'.

Going into residential care

Anticipation It will come as no surprise to find that the elderly people interviewed had varying ideas about what going into residential care would be like. Some longed for a refuge and a respite from their day to day problems of struggling to live in the community. Others feared harsh regulations and the nature of other residents' attitudes and disabilities.

'I would like to feel free both physically and mentally, but to have somebody to call upon if I wanted help or advice. Somebody just to buck me up. To put it blunt I like someone just to make a fuss of me as I go along through the day. You see I have been on my own so much'.

'My brother's in a very nice home in Maidstone, it seems more like a hotel. You're warm there aren't you? They're centrally heated aren't they? I mean here I don't think the winter is very good for me here, I don't really'.

'Well I think it will be a change from getting into a bedroom and to a sitting room, won't it. Then moving into having your meals somewhere else, you wouldn't have your meals in a sitting room would you? I'd be amongst people, shouldn't I? There must be some nice people, mustn't there?'

'Of course I would miss my own home. Doing things, well what shall I say, having things when I want them etc, I mean we know in these homes you must go by rules and regulations, and I would enjoy the early morning cup of tea and that sort of thing and the meals in general, but still I don't like parting with things around me, if you understand'.

'No I'm trying to forget about it, I'm trying not to think about it, because I think all kinds of things, and well, in hospital you meet all kinds, and some of the old people, poor things, I mean such as dribbling when they're having their meals and all things like that. I think I shall be sitting next to them and everything like that.'

'If you went into a home you have got to abide with what they do, well that is my opinion. I do not know whether that is right or wrong, but I mean they are very kind I believe, very kind. I hear very good reports and that you have your tea at a certain time. I don't know whether they let you have it any other time, I don't suppose they do. If you are there you have to have it'.

'Well the thing is I can't expect anything, can I? If I go in a home there's rules and regulations, least I expect there are, but it would be nice if I could make a cup of tea when I needed it. I would like that, but then would that be possible?'

'I'd be warmer if I get into a nice place, but if there are people talking a lot of rubbish all day long I'd think myself I'd be going loopy'.

'Well, if I could get a room, which I think it's the impossible, downstairs, but then I do not say I would not mix with the other people round about, but you could guarantee your little room and have your own little wireless on, your little television on and be like that instead of being in a mass.

'For one thing, I didn't know it was going to be such a place full of mental people. I mean these people are really mental. Some of them are dirty in their habits. It isn't that I object it might have been a relation of mine, who knows, but I think this should have been put clearer.'

'Once I think some years ago I went to visit a home outside Brighton, and was really horrifying to me, I don't want to give up this, but what am I going to do? See I'm eighty six and eighty seven on my next birthday.

'Well the thing is if I go into a home I shall have to give up this, shouldn't I? It's going to be quite different. I shall lose my independence'.

Striking a bargain Whereas some of the group anticipated having to relinquish most things on entering a home others adopted a more bargaining attitude. They felt that if they put up with some things they did not much like they might be allowed to hang on to cherished possessions or have some leverage in other directions.

'I've got a record player here. I would like to take that if I could. If I couldn't, well I just simply can't. I'm not going to be dogmatic about anything, just simply say this if anybody is going to try and help me I am willing to accept it. The only thing is I would like a little bit of say in it – not all the other sides, a little bit of my side as well. That's all. I haven't got much here, no furniture. If I want something I go and ask, which is very rare, because I want so little.

That's the trouble of people trying to help, their difficult side of the question is how can I help? But the most difficult side of the question is what do I want help for? I may be all right, I'm not feeling too bad now, although I can hardly walk with my legs, but another time I may be really off colour, then I'm afraid. I'm not too bad when I'm off colour, I get ratty about it'.

'Well there's one or two little bits that I'll be contented not to take, I don't mind forfeiting a lot of things if I can go somewhere relatively comfortable and feel that I'm being looked after'.

How admission to residential care came about Elderly people were admitted to residential care by a variety of different means. Sometimes they brought up the subject of admission, but it was frequently first mentioned by a relative or an official. Often there was a sense of inevitability about it all.

'It was my son's idea. I was not well and I did not seem able to be looking after myself, for instance having my dinners and that sort of thing, and he asked the social worker to find out about it and asked me, he would not do anything, he would not force me to go but he wants me to say I will go, but I have not said that I would go. Because I do not like the idea. When I was not well I had rather bad falls, I have had several very bad falls, in fact I cracked my head twice, I wonder I have got any brain up there at all. I fall, unsteady, very unsteady. Well the doctor did suggest to the social worker that I should go into a home'.

'Well I think candidly it was myself and the doctor. I was feeling so ill that I just didn't feel that I could manage, but now I'm feeling so much better that the thought of going into a home is horrifying to me'.

'Well she came, so the doctor said would I like to go into a welfare home? So she said of course you will lose your independence. I said I'm thinking. But she said you can't look after yourself. I've no alternative.

'It was talked over between the committee and the doctor. You see they do no nursing and it was getting to the stage where I wanted help more and so I put my name down, enquired about five different places and with my doctor's help this is the one that came out. I had a home help coming in to do the room but there were certain things getting too much. I couldn't do it. Because you see I've got it in my hands, this arthritis – I couldn't manage.

'I did have the doctor send his welfare visitor to me, and she said she couldn't understand why I wanted to go to a home because she said, you're intelligent. I said my brain's all right, I'm not senile, nothing like that but I said I'm physically unsuited to do for myself, and I said I'm quite contented to go into a home.

'Well then it got so my arthritis got worse and I used to have my own room you see and I couldn't manage it any more. So I told Sister Theresa. She said "It is your own decision – it's your decision that you're going". So I said "Yes, at eighty three, I can't carry on you see.'

'My friend wouldn't have me back, so I went to my sister. . . . My sister put me in here. . . . '

External pressure applied to get the elderly person to accept admission to residential care Pressure, subtle or overt, was felt by some to have been applied to achieve compliance with a plan for admission to a home, and admission was seen by most as final and irreversible.

'They wouldn't let me go back there to look after myself, so they put me in a home. This is where they put me. The social worker said I should come here. She wouldn't let me go back to look after myself. She said "No, you can't go back there and look after yourself. We'll find you a home". You see, so this is where they found me. I was on my own in Brighton. I'd got nobody in Brighton, you see. No, I couldn't really (say no to the social worker), because I'd got nowhere to go, you see'.

'They arranged it, the sister and that you know. She suddenly pounced on me one day. I was coming here on the Thursday. Told me at the beginning of the week'.

'I think it was the doctor's idea at the hospital. He and the sister spoke to me about going into a home. Would I be happier, they thought'.

Information given to applicant about residential care prior to admission Considering that the people concerned were undertaking a very major change in their lives (that of giving up living independently) their lack of information about their future home was often remarkable.

'I didn't know as much as I know now. I think things should have been put clearer. I feel we should have been told a bit more about it. I should still have come I suppose'.

'I don't think they told me what it would be like'.

'Yes, but I tell you the truth I thought they'd have card games and all that, but they don't. They just talk to one another'.

'Oh no, no. They told me there'd always be someone to look after me, because that's what I was worried about. I can't do everything for myself, but anyway they assured me the staff here don't mind'.

'I was supposed to be going to a welfare home where people have their own little sitting rooms and they're completely on their own except for a communal dining room. That's what I wanted. That's what I was told'.

'No, I didn't know what they was going to be like. No I didn't know what to expect'.

'I'd heard all about it, (from) several people who'd got relatives in here'.

'She said she thought I'd be happier than in hospital'.

Preferred lifestyles Some had ideas of their own about where they would like to live. In practice these would not always have proved realistic because they tended to overestimate their relatives' or friends' desire to be involved in their care.

'It was really very nice – I had my own room, television. I had a front room over the sea. I was very happy there, the food was good and I was very happy there but I couldn't stay there any longer because of the expense'.

'I've got a sister living in Coldean, that's why I want to get to this home you see – at Coldean (sheltered flatlets) – so I could be near her and we could go out together'.

'Well I would rather I went into digs. Actually, my wish would be that I went back to Birmingham. I've got quite a number of friends round Birmingham, who I think would have put me up – No, I didn't tell the social worker, not at the time. Naturally I thought when they said about going into a home I thought I should pay a

normal fee; because I should have to pay a normal fee if I was in digs'.

Visits made by applicants to prospective homes before admission It was rare for applicants to have visited the residential establishment before admission, but one or two had done so and had comments to make about the experience.

'I've been to one home to see them, all sitting round, no interest at all. Well I am not like that, I like to be a little bit capable, I know I am not so young as most of them.'

'Yes this lady that came from the welfare took me to see two of them. Just to have a look at them. One I thought was too posh, it was a new one it was more like going into a hotel – so posh it didn't seem homely somehow, of course you can't just tell looking round, might be all right when you're there'.

'We've stayed there – its a wonderful place, the staff there are all nice. It's run on such a wonderful line, they all work together in such a wonderful way'.

Loss of home

Not surprisingly losing their homes and a lifetime's possessions were desolating experiences.

'I parted with my home. I practically gave my home away to live along with this sister-in-law. I didn't want to come but I wouldn't go against my wife. The specialist said it would do her good, I didn't want to stand in her way, I'd rather see her get better than stand in her way. I wouldn't stand in her way under no circumstances. She only lived nine weeks. . . . My wife died in nine weeks and left me stranded, you see'.

'So my sister and her daughter and her husband, they said, "Well, it's silly, you still paying rent on that flat". They said, "You won't be able to go back there again". So of course, what they've done they've sold up a lot of my furniture and taken what they wanted themselves and just one or two little bits they think I might want if I ever get this bed-sitting room or whatever it is. My sister's got most of my clothes because I won't have any here, only just what I'm wearing'.

'No, I didn't bring any furniture with me. I didn't know I could. No my sister's got it all. I left it, gave it to her – Oh yes, I've got a big cupboard with a medicine chest on top'.

'Oh no. My daughter's saved some, an armchair and a carpet and a few odds and ends. She's got them in her home. Well there'd be no room here, not having my own bedroom'.

'No I couldn't bring my chair. I left that at the convent. I left everything at the convent. Bits of furniture I valued my cousins have taken to keep for me. Well they can have it I shan't want it again, but still they prefer not to, I think. I brought my television, which is portable, one of those tables which slide under the bed and a nest of bookshelves. No back and the books are always tumbling out. Well I would have liked some of it (my furniture) – It was very nice, very very old furniture, antique. I don't think it would have suited this house. It would have looked terribly shabby. But I would have liked, yes probably, one or two little things'.

'No, sadly no. I asked (the social worker) about that because I had been told you couldn't bring anything, any furniture or anything like that. And he said "No, you can't. They might let you bring your electric clock". Which was a presentation clock and so all my silver wedding presents, my golden wedding presents all had to go. You see there's no room, nowhere to put them. I had to get rid of everything. Mostly distributed among friends. I've been assured any day I should want them I can have them'.

'Well no, I didn't want to bring anything'.

'My furniture's been sold....My son sold it'.

Being in residential care

Once admitted to a residential home the details of the day to day routine and domestic arrangements assumed enormous importance.

Room sharing There was some confusion about whether residents would have a room of their own or share with others.

'They told me when I came here I should have my own room. Well that was all right. When I got here, "Did I mind sharing a room with a lady for two nights?" Here I am still sharing with her (three months later)'.

'I thought I should have my own room and I had it when I first came and I should like it now'.

Daily routine Early rising was not disliked by some. Activity on the whole was welcomed, with bedmaking more common, and more acceptable, than laying tables for meals.

'(I get up) fairly early, I should think.... Just right. When they come, you see, they bring a cup of tea and then I get up.... I don't want to go to bed late either'.

'We have to get up about seven. (Is it seven?) I don't know. I'm always used to getting up early'.

'Well I go and help them wash up and I keep the room dusted and that'.

'Oh yes I make my own bed, Mary and I, we make our own beds. No we don't do anything like that (laying the table) I couldn't be bothered doing anything like that'.

'Oh yes I make my bed and dust my room. No I don't (lay the table) I can't stand you see'.

'No I don't make my bed but I can. They do it. I strip it so that it can be aired. I could easily do it, it wouldn't be any trouble, if they wanted me to. I don't know if they do, do they?

'I find the hours are very long, I get very tired. I don't seem as if I can catch up on sleep. You see it's noise. The other house was as silent as the grave, with few people in. There's not a lot of people and you all have your own rooms but (here) from the time you're roused, half past five, with the tea trolleys getting ready, there's no quiet. It seems all noise.'

Bathing On the whole it was accepted that help with bathing was necessary and many residents had been used to the district nurse visiting to help them with this at home.

'There's men on here, you see and they come and fill the bath and I've always managed to bath myself. They come in several times to see. As a rule they help me (to get in and out) because as I say I've been a bit tottery since I was ill. But otherwise they're all right to me, they just help me to get in the bath and I bath myself and then they come in and they'll just help me to stand up in the bath and leave me to do the rest, on my own I'm all right, you see, I'm all right then. It gives you more confidence when they help you like that a little bit'.

'No I couldn't bath, no. Oh they're very good. They've got every equipment'.

'Yes, I bath myself. Well, they have come but I don't want them. I can do it myself. They have come when I'm in the bath and that, but not always. No I don't want any help. I can help myself in everything like that'.

'Well, the matron always helps us. Oh no (I can't manage on my own) because I've got this (bad leg). She's very nice'.

'Oh they bath me. I can't get in the bath by myself. Before I know what I'm doing I'm in the bath. They know how to do it, don't they? They sit me on a chair and I seem to slide in. They're lovely people here'.

Food Mealtimes assume particular importance in residential homes. The groups appeared to tolerate the food and the times of meals rather than finding any active pleasure in them.

'Well the food is very good. I will say that, it's very good but really there's not enough of it for me. I've got a good appetite'.

'Well you get a place like this where there's about forty people you've got a job to please everybody. I've heard them "I don't want that. . . ." But there is things as I'm not too keen on but I don't grumble, I just carry on. Such things as spam and things like that, that I am not very keen on'.

'Do you know, every day, every week, for weeks and weeks and weeks we were served last. We had our food and it was stone cold. Really I got so wild about it, I did ask, "Couldn't someone else have a turn of it". It's got so bad lately and I can't understand it we've got everything up to date in the kitchen, supposed to be, hot plates, everything'.

'That's a long time from tea. You see you have tea. It used to be from four o'clock. Then you've nothing more until next morning. If breakfast is late, as it is sometimes, it's half past eight before you get another mouthful. That's a very big number of hours'.

Mobility Mobility on the part of residents was limited and there was anxiety about not being able to manage if venturing far afield. The speed with which the lift doors opened and shut, particularly when there was a rush of people trying to get to the dining room, was the cause of much apprehension.

'To me the lift shuts too quickly again. It's been speeded up a bit I think. You get three people with zimmers, a person with sticks, a person with crutches. You've only so many seconds before that door automatically shuts. I feel it all over every time I go in'.

'There's such a rush for the lift. It's awfully awkward in the morning. You see those people who are lucky enough to get the lift put someone to hold the button on the top. It goes down to the bottom, misses our floor, and goes back up to the top. It goes down to the bottom. Do you know I've stood there for a quarter of an hour in the morning when I've only just got up and I'm simply full of pain – I've told him and he said "I can't see that anything can be done".'

'Oh well I couldn't do any stairs. Really that was one of the assets. I get early to meals because I can get the lift quickly. If I leave it until five or ten minutes before a meal I get stranded there. Can't get a lift you see, they get full. It gets full. Yes I'm quite au fait with it now. I can press the buttons, I watched the old people. I thought well if these old dears at ninety seven can manage it, so can I'.

'Oh yes I can go out, but I've had this bad turn just lately that I haven't gone out. I'm rather fond of walking and if I can walk I'll walk, I won't ride'.

'No I'm not safe enough to go out. I go out with my children, they come and take me out in the car, Sundays and that, out to lunch and I come back after tea time'.

'My son comes every week....Can't go out with them weather like this. I hope to (in the summer). I don't want to (go out in the minibus)'.

'I came here on the 11th October and I've been in the minibus once but that was my fault. When I first came here I was so sure that I wouldn't be able to get in the bus that I refused.

'Then Ron said to me once, he said, "Are you coming with us?" I said "No, I can't get on" He said, "Oh you can". He helped me on the bus, to get up those little steps.'

'Not much. You see my sight is not too good and another thing I'm not very fond of going out much'.

Pensions and payments The amount which should be contributed by a resident towards her keep was a bone of contention as well as a matter for some confusion.

'Well, I didn't know it until I came but I did hand it (pension book) over, and I also had to, which I think was going rather far. I had to sign another form which gave them access to my bank account and my money which I have in the Alliance Building – and what else had I in the bank?....No I did not, no I didn't (know I'd have to do this). I've heard since this is illegal that they couldn't make you. Somebody came and took it up with their solicitor and they definitely would not let them have it. I didn't mind that much. I told the truth. It would have been nice to know my rights'.

'No, I didn't know what they were going to charge me. I'm really a bit disappointed over the charge. No I didn't know before I came'.

'Well I had two pension books, a war pension book and my own, which was in my own right. Well when I came here I gave up one pension book, my state pension book and I said to my sister "Look you keep this other pension book for me. Go and draw the pension every Monday because I don't want them to think at the Ministry of Pensions I've no need of it – and then put it in with my savings".'

'The home has the pension. Oh I have £2 per week pocket money. That's quite sufficient for me'.

'I don't deal with the money part, only having my pocket money. My nephew does all that'.

'They've got it here – They give me £3 a week. Can I break in about that? Well, you see, I've got my income tax to pay and my ordinary account is closed to make a cheque account. Well I've written to say I must have a cheque book because I must pay income tax. It was due on the first, wasn't it? Well I don't suppose they've had time to do anything about it but I think I'll write to the Trustees Savings Bank and ask them to send me a cheque. I can't bear to owe anything'.

'I don't get a pension dear....I don't draw a pension dear but I don't know how I get it....No, they don't give me any money. They pay my expenses I think'.

'Me and my wife worked hard for 60 years and saved, with the idea that we shouldn't sponge on anybody when I retired. Well she died in nine weeks and I automatically took her share of the savings, which made it actually worse under the Welfare. I'm paying practically £38 per week, which I think is a bit, well my savings will soon go at that rate. What I think is wrong, I think the system is wrong all together. Because there's people in here, you take a woman who's got a bungalow. She sells the bungalow through her son or daughter, in their name, and the money's banked. And so she'll draw £50 or anything like that, when she likes, which actually according to the Welfare she's got no money you see'.

'They're getting more from me than anyone else I'm sure, in this home. They've got both my pensions'.

After admission Once the drama and crisis of admission are forgotten monotony can readily take over.

'I haven't been well since I've been here really'.

'I'm quite happy, very happy here, I am. Everyone's so kind, they're always ready to help you'.

'They take away your dignity bit by bit'.

'I just sit around and read or have the television'.

'I'd go mad without my knitting'.

'Yes I'm happy....Well if I had a nice – a person like myself to share. Oh I can't say it. You'll guess, you'll guess, you'll guess'.

'I don't feel at all happy here. I feel that I shouldn't be here with all these old people. I'm not old, I'm not old, and I shouldn't be here in this home. I mean, they're all much older than me. Why should I be here with them?'

'My friends would soon have something to say if there was anything wrong. But the other poor souls, there's so many of them got nobody'.

'I can't read, I'm going blind. I can't watch television. So my radio is my life, what I'd do without it I don't know'.

'You can look at one side of it and say ''No, they don't care'' but in another way they care all the time'.

Rights and status

'You have to accept what they say' The matter of what rights and status residents have is a fundamental one. The elderly people interviewed appeared to consider that they had to do as they were told and that they had little command over their own destinies. Things tended to happen to them with little explanation.

'Who told me to call them matron? No-one, but everybody does'.

'I had to sign another form which gave them access to my bank account'.

'Here, you can't do the same as you can in your own home. You see, I used to bathe my eyes night and morning. It must be sterilised water and lotion, you see. Well I can't do it here – Well I suppose I could if I had the boiling water but I don't like to bother them'.

'He came to see me when I'd been here two days. He said ''I'm sorry Mrs Gully, you won't be under me any longer. You're out of my district. You'll be under Dr X''. Well I never had the faintest idea who Dr X was. Goodness me, when I saw this Dr X I thought to myself well I don't want you for my doctor'.

'One thing I have found, the greatest disadvantage of the lot. It's got a lot of advantages. I'm not grumbling. It's the lack of privacy. There isn't an inch where you have privacy. They never knock on the door, they barge in, any time and any how, and really sometimes your bedroom is all you've got. You can understand. You see there's no lock anywhere as you'll realise, and unless someone knocks then you've no minute of privacy ever, not ever. Up to a little while ago children were roaming around from the school, they came in and ran in when they liked. They came barging into your room, no matter if you're laying down trying to get a bit of sleep in the afternoon. Four of them, perhaps five. I've had as many as five in that little room'.

'When I first came here the welfare woman was a bit cheeky. She said ''you've got to pay, if you don't pay you've got to go to court and jail''. Which I think was wrong'.

'I've been having these pills for eleven years and nothing's ever gone wrong. It's the waiting for them. Now when I go away on holiday, I went away for a week's holiday, they gave me them all. They trusted me then. It seems when you're quite sane and you've been taking them all these years and you realise exactly what they are and what they're for, you ought to be trusted. It's for them to judge I think'.

Could things be changed? Opinions varied about whether or not it was possible to alter the way things are.

'I honestly believe if you'd got a complaint, if I'd got a complaint and went to the Matron, I honestly believe that she'd do her best to put it right'.

'I don't think they would like that. I've never heard of anything like it. In fact you're not encouraged. Things go on that no-one knows anything about, and I've noticed'.

Taking part in shaping your world – the Residents' Conference The first Residents' Conference was held in Brighton in 1977, and since then has become an annual feature. It is an important development, as it provides residents with a forum for sharing their opinions with those from other homes, as well as an opportunity for a direct exchange of views with staff who are responsible for running the homes. These conferences produce lively discussion and it is interesting to contrast the views expressed there with those brought up by the groups of elderly people interviewed at the beginning of the project.

In order to provide an idea of the nature of these conferences some of the main themes emerging from the 1978 Residents' Conference are summarised here. Sixty residents from fifteen homes for the elderly in Brighton met with social services department staff and five county councillors.

General points Residents agreed that they felt quite happy with the standard of living in the homes at present. They hoped that more mixed homes would gradually be introduced and that there would be much greater dissemination of information within and between the homes. The title 'old people's home' was cordially disliked and names like 'retired persons' home' or 'elderly persons' home' were preferred.

Admissions and reviews Entry into a home was sometimes felt to be a great shock, and it was suggested that there should be a one week trial period prior to full admission. This initial period of residence was felt by all to be a particularly testing time for residents. It would be desirable for more information to be provided about routine and about activities available.

Few residents considered themselves to be familiar with the review system, and they thought they should have the right to attend their own reviews. There was much support for this suggestion.

Group living The idea of group living had a mixed reception. It was defined in this project as a situation where small groups of about 8–10 residents shared a living space for sitting and eating purposes, and took part in washing up and simple food preparation, whilst sharing some communal facilities in the home with other groups. Most residents liked the idea in principle but they had reservations about how it worked out in practice, particularly in small homes where there were a large number of confused residents and staffing ratios were not good.

Those residents already taking part in group living were in favour of it; though the more active members felt some resentment of the frail or confused members who, they felt, should receive more help from staff. Placing confused residents in homes specially catering for them was discussed but did not receive general support. On the other hand group living helped the more able residents to develop independence.

Food More flexibility in the content of the meals was hoped for and it was thought that this might reduce wastage. Most residents enjoyed the food provided but would like more choice.

Social activities It was felt that many of the talents possessed by the residents were going to waste. For instance a number had skills in such things as gardening and craftwork. It was thought that open days to show and sell garden produce and articles made by residents would provide a stimulus and could increase contact with the community. Another means of enabling the able bodied to become more connected with the local community might be to develop such activities as bingo evenings, snooker and card and darts leagues. There was much support for more entertainment in the homes in the shape of film shows and talks, and staff agreed that these could easily be arranged.

There was very strong support for the proposal that in homes having no pub within easy reach a bar should be opened. There was also a request that a coin operated telephone should be installed in each home as this would enable residents to contact their relatives and friends more easily.

There was a request for more outings and some residents professed a willingness to organise these for themselves. Staff, however, said they had found it extremely difficult to get sufficient residents to go on outings, and many had been planned which subsequently had to be abandoned.

Transport and holidays Residents felt they would like to have more opportunity to travel, visit friends and relations and go into town. Two problems made these activities difficult for them: lack of transport and lack of money. They thought the first could be relieved by having more voluntary helpers. Allowances, they thought, had not kept pace with inflation and this made longer journeys and holidays difficult. Brighton Transport, for instance, would only permit a certain number of tokens to be used for individual journeys and long journeys had to be paid for in part by residents. It was felt that allowances for residents going on holiday should be on a pro rata basis and not, as now, £14 per week and £3.50 for part of a week.

Reference

[1]*Patterns of Care for the Elderly: Part II,* available on request from the Development Group, DHSS, Alexander Fleming House, Elephant & Castle, London SE1 6BY.

'I had to be fed and I hated it. It was an uncomfortable experience both physically and emotionally'.

Setting the scene – a role play

It takes a great leap of the imagination for most of us to begin to understand what the day-to-day business of being old and in residential care can be like. We are outsiders looking in. It is equally difficult to comprehend the stresses which residential staff inevitably experience in their day-to-day work.

In order to facilitate the process of understanding and to heighten the impact of the material received from the elderly people in interviews (see Chapter One) it was decided early on in the project to stage a role play. In order to experience time hanging heavily the exercise lasted four hours. A lunch period was included and this brought home to the participants the problems of communal living and the different viewpoints of staff and residents.

Despite the fact that the exercise took place in an artificial environment the participants found it an illuminating experience, and for most it was unexpectedly tiring.

Dr. Tom Douglas, Senior Lecturer, University of Keele, conducted the exercise and his introduction is as he gave it at the time, as are the comments on the experience which follow.

Introduction to the exercise by Tom Douglas

'In this simulation exercise I would ask you to use your imagination in order to learn. One method of learning is experiential – that is, "being" and "doing", and I suggest that for four hours you play parts as residents and staff in homes for the elderly. Because it is far from easy to get elderly people to tell us how they feel and react, we are going to put ourselves in their place in order to experience for ourselves what their problems can be. This is an hotel, not a home for the elderly. The dining room is served by waitresses and the physical environment is in many respects unsuited to the exercise. But by being honest and sincere in the use of your imagination, by treating it as a serious enterprise and the time as valuable learning time, I think it can work. Try to feel in every fibre of your being; become the person you choose to play.

'Use your own experience of contact with elderly people, of films, TV or any other source to act out their behaviour patterns, likes, dislikes, idiosyncrasies and disabilities. It is natural you will feel anxious about this, but remember that residents also are anxious, especially at key times, of which admission is one.

'Your own lives are full of options; for the next few hours your options will be limited – you will soon discover how far! When in the future we plan for what we think elderly residents might like, this exercise will perhaps assist in recalling how limited their range of choice has really become.

'Each of the three groups is asked to imagine itself to be in a unit of thirty in the main day room of a home for the elderly. The first half-hour should be used to plan how you are to function, what kind of residents you are and whether you are to include day care. Try to choose roles you do not yourselves fill in your working life, as far away from your everyday occupation as you can make it.

'A "major happening" is allocated to each group, though these will no doubt be supplemented by other events springing from the dynamics of each situation and the inventiveness of members.

Group 1 will admit two new residents;

Group 2 will have two members who leave to be cared for by relatives;

Group 3 will have a resident who is terminally ill and dies.

'Coffee will arrive at 11.10. By then you should be "in role" and must cope with serving it.

'Disability aids such as wheelchairs, walking aids, bandages and some special clothing are provided. Earplugs (to simulate deafness), arm slings, crutches and second hand clothing are also available. Lunch will be taken in role. The hotel staff have been briefed and you will find if you behave like an elderly person they will in fact treat you like one!

'The length of the exercise is deliberate; it is necessary for it to last long enough for you to begin at least to experience the fact that time is the enemy of the elderly resident. Brief role play will in no way yield full learning about the lives of elderly residents, for whom the passage of time becomes a dominant factor in their lives. Boredom, by its very nature, needs time to be fully experienced. Only through a sufficiently long passage of time and events can one appreciate the everyday experience of the person whose role you assume.

'After the simulation, we will gather in plenary session to exchange our reactions, feelings and insights. Experiential learning is a very active method – it is not passive acceptance of information handed out by experts. It focuses on the active participation by the individual and aims to deepen insight and broaden understanding. Without doubt the level of success depends on the intensity of participation, both for the individual and the group as a whole.'

The exercise The three groups each used their preparatory half-hour quite differently, and thus from the very beginning each 'home' took on a distinctive personality. In some degree this resulted from the impact of particular members on the others; for example, a particularly bossy care assistant full of organising zeal generated a good deal of activity which was not very purposeful; one exceedingly neurotic, attention-seeking resident caused repeated disruption which sparked off hostility, irritation and a sense of constant crisis; a quartet of very apathetic disabled residents spread around them an aura of hopelessness which seemed as infectious as measles: some caught it and others shunned them.

As the morning progressed it was very evident that each 'home' had already acquired individual characteristics and that these could easily harden into persisting patterns of behaviour, becoming ritualised in both form and content. That this could happen in only a few hours indicates the nature of the task confronting departments wishing to change the style and quality of relationships amongst groups of staff and residents which have been in existence for some time.

Lack of privacy The large groups of thirty occupying one sitting room were universally condemned by all the participants. They all felt on top of one another. There was no chance for any privacy and most simply felt they could not remain long in the lounge with the press of people of different personalities and idiosyncrasies.

Sometimes there was a good deal of ambivalence about staff. On the one hand they were never there when wanted; on the other there was resentment at the seemingly ever-watchful eye. 'You can't even go to the lavatory without somebody taking note of it'. A need to escape manifested itself in various ways: withdrawal into defensive silence, restless movement about the limited corridors, suggestions to go out for walks or day trips. Perhaps the worst overall effect was that lack of sufficient 'territory' and privacy generated petty antagonisms and aggressive attitudes which militated against mutual help and tended to create an 'us and them' feeling towards staff.

Arbitrary actions of staff, lack of choice Particular resentment was expressed in relation to arbitrary actions by staff. Most evident was the way the TV was switched on without consultation, the noise level turned up or down, and equally abruptly, programmes were switched off in mid-sentence. For those not interested in the programme it thus became an intrusive background jabber; to those listening it spoilt their concentration and enjoyment. In its own way this was symbolic of the general imposition of other people's decisions and of residents' lack of choice. At least those able to walk could remove themselves into the corridor, but many had to find their own means of enduring it as there was no alternative.

Boredom, apathy, suppressed feelings The majority experienced a sence of enervating boredom attributed to a variety of factors, of which lack of purposeful activity was only one. 'Activities' in themselves sometimes had little meaning; one lady was endlessly dusting the corridor windows, because it was her 'job for the morning'. Conversation itself could turn into an exchange of platitudes without real feelings or communication. Coupled with the boredom was a sense of 'loneliness among the crowd', of being locked into oneself by circumstances. Several complained that it proved impossible to make anyone really listen to what they were trying to say, especially if they had some speech impairment or were in failing health. 'Yes, dear' from staff in a soothing voice could be enraging if you were, as one expressed it, 'trying to prove I was not entirely senile, that I had a point of view and wanted to express it'. One resident played the role of a difficult and aggressive man, always provoking a verbal sparring match with others, and with one fellow resident in particular. 'But when he left, we missed him'.

It seemed to be generally agreed that noisiness, aggression and disruptive and bizarre behaviour were means of provoking interest and securing attention. 'If you were quiet and understanding, nobody took much notice of you as a person'. The boredom was coupled with immobile apathy among some residents who sat silently around the walls gazing vacantly into space. Yet snatches of conversation or utterance aimed at nobody in particular gave clues to intense inner feelings or suppressed loneliness, hopelessness or grief. The following is a selection of random comments illustrating this theme.

'I don't belong in here. My daughter ought to take me out of it. She'll come one day.'

'My husband always used to say, "You've got lovely soft hair – don't let it go". Now look at me'.

'Matron, matron, I feel like crying'.

'I miss my garden. I'd be planting it all out now'.

'Get us a bottle of Guinness, miss. I do miss my Guinness before dinner. Nobody gets it for me'.

'You going out there? Well, its something to do, isn't it?'

'Yes I see you have your little walk'.

'You are *you*, then? People here come in and out and never say anything or explain who they are. You might as well not exist for all the notice they take'.

'They sold all my things; everything. I only brought a photo of my wife and I keep that tucked away. It's all I've got now'.

A deaf resident in a wheelchair commented: 'My dependence on others was dreadful. I had to wait so long for everything and although at first people tried to talk to me I couldn't really hear. More talking and the background noise seemed to produce an even greater feeling of isolation. In the end I just gave up. I was too tired even to try to hear or to communicate'.

No doubt in their efforts to get into role seminar members tended to emphasise many of the more negative responses they had heard or observed among the elderly. But it was significant that, over and above the assumed roles and reactions, genuine feelings emerged which were generated by the powerful situation. This was especially true of the boredom and frustration, the feeling of impotence to change the situation, and the resentment of some members of the staff.

Staff attitudes Those taking on staff roles seemed exhausted by their experiences. They commented that a great deal of their effort to make people physically comfortable and clean brought little in the way of spontaneous thanks or response. In this exercise the residents on the whole tended to be resistant to staff intervention, thus providing an artificially enhanced experience of frustration among staff. 'They don't respond when you *do* try', was one comment.

The need to combine general care with attention to visitors, major events such as death or new admissions, unexpected crises, outbursts and arguments, created a tiring and worrying time. Members who were not employed in homes for the elderly said it gave them a new respect for the stamina and skills required in residential care. One commented, 'To me, ninety-five per cent of residents seemed either apathetic or aggressive in some way. They were not pleased with our efforts to assist, nor did they offer to help'.

The mid-day meal Some time before the hour of serving the meal, the process of 'toiletting' began. With the varied disabilities and some residents in wheelchairs, this was quite a lengthy ritual, working up to one of the major events of the day, the consumption of a main meal. Televisions were switched off, staff bustled about and residents were marshalled in procession.

In the hotel, the route from group rooms to the central dining room was a difficult one. Some had to negotiate stairs or lifts, and all had to pass through narrow corridors and a large kitchen, which is unlikely to be the case in any residential establishment. However, the fact that nearly a hundred people were converging on the dining room for a meal at a set hour provided an enhanced example of the levels of tension and frustration which this sort of event can provoke, as it is one of the highlights of the day in many establishments.

The procession wound slowly forward and provoked genuine (as well as simulated) feelings of irritation and impatience. There was much maneouvring of wheelchairs, some pushing and shoving, and criticisms of residents who lagged behind too much or got in the way of the more active. Everyone commented on the way they suddenly found themselves becoming selfish and anxious to push ahead no matter who was around.

'I knew I'd got to get there somehow, no matter who else got pushed aside'.

'I don't want to get stuck behind her – she always holds up everybody'.

It was also an occasion for criticisms about other residents, often expressed obliquely but within the hearing of the person concerned.

'She's a bit upset, she thinks her daughter is going to leave her instead of just for the day. She always makes a fuss'.

'He's a bit hopeless – in a state today'.

'I've had just about enough of him this morning. I'm glad to get away. Always making a commotion he is'.

Another feeling which rose to the surface was one of helplessness, when confronted with minor setbacks or some of the disturbances created by a few residents, because of the tedious nature of the process. There were numerous calls for matron or other staff members, and complaints when nobody appeared instantly to help. Certainly there was a good deal of quite mutual assistance, usually accompanied by remarks intended to be encouraging, but somehow these simply drew attention to the incapacity of the person being helped. One resident fell out of his chair, but he had to be left temporarily lying on the floor and was told somebody would be back with him in a minute, while the procession moved inexorably forward. Again, it is unlikely that these circumstances would be reproduced in a home in quite the same form, but the basic feelings evoked reflected members' own observations of what they saw happening in everyday life.

During the meal, a high proportion of members stayed most remarkably in role at the cost of considerable discomfort and stress. This particularly applied to those playing the part of severely handicapped residents in wheelchairs or senile patients unable to take much initiative in feeding themselves. Around the dining room, one could discern a whole array of attitudes, ranging from those sitting meekly waiting for someone to feed them, those quietly getting on with eating what they could, those demanding attention, making a noise or displaying eccentric behaviour. A few complained continuously about the food, service or other residents.

The aftermath Inevitably, during the aftermath to the role play, people tended to describe those experiences which most deeply affected their view of ways of caring for the elderly or attitudes towards them. Alongside the negatives were the expressions of pleasure at efforts to help each other, the understanding of personal limitations and the patience displayed by those undertaking staff roles.

The planned and unplanned incidents of the role play seemed to be artificial events in themselves, yet they provoked much thought and discussion afterwards, as members found themselves confronted with situations they had not previously experienced. For example, a staff member who took the role of a patient suffering from a terminal illness was deeply affected. The person who assumed the role of matron receiving new admissions was confronted by difficult situations without having familiar patterns of behaviour to guide her through. The major incidents were the deaths of two residents, the admissions of two residents to one group and the discharge from another of two who left to live with relatives. There were also two accidents which caused considerable crises, including one unplanned event when somebody got firmly stuck in a wheelchair. Retrospectively the value of these aspects of the role play lay in the capacity of members to reflect on the situations and to compare them with similar events in the everyday running of their own establishments.

Mealtimes Many commented on the importance assumed by the meal as the day's main event, and thought that the size of the gathering gave it a disproportionate degree of difficulty. It would have been much more relaxed to have had the meal in the small groups and would have cut out a good deal of the lengthy preliminary processes.

'I found the meal very difficult. Half-way through I could eat no more even with help. Because of my disabilities, I simply could not be bothered to eat the rest, although I was still hungry'.

'I had to be fed and I hated it. It was an uncomfortable experience both physically and emotionally, although everybody including the waitress joined in and were very helpful'.

'I selected what I knew I could handle easily with my disabilities, although in fact they were really things I didn't like very much'.

'My daughter is ever such a good cook. Before I came in here, she used to make all my meals'.

'My husband always loved his roast beef and Yorkshire pud. He used to say nobody made it like I did'.

'We always had our dinner at night, when the boys came in from work'.

Conversation also included speculation about the afternoon and how it was to be spent, including debate about going on outings. There were few incidents during the meal, most people concentrating their energies on the process of consuming food. Those who found they were unable to sustain the role were easily spotted, as they were visibly eating like much younger people. The staff of the hotel responded enthusiastically to the situation, helping to cut up meat, but they fell into the trap of asking people at tables to 'hold up their hands' for a choice of sweet and other courses.

The members acting as staff experienced the discomfort of trying to eat their own food whilst at the same time helping or feeding others.

Admissions to the homes New residents arriving went out of their way to display all the characteristics of anxiety expressed in fear, rejection and hostility. One deaf man arrived complete with imaginary ferret and budgie. The social worker who introduced him had evidently said he might be able to have them, and he was busily engaged throughout in coping with his anger at the prospect of being parted from them. At the time of his arrival, there were no senior staff available and a care assistant clearly could not be responsible for the major decision involved. What emerged from this was the uncertainty about the home's attitude towards pets and the lack of information before admission.

A new lady resident was mourning the loss of her home including her furniture and 'all her little things around her'. She reacted by a series of statements: that she was not going to have a bath straightaway; she was not going to share a room; she did not know anybody and was not likely to stay very long.

A point which occurred both during the admissions and in general conversation was the wish for a single room, the expectation that it would be available, and resentment at having to share with a stranger.

From these episodes, the main points emerging were the necessity for adequate preparation, realistic and correct knowledge of what was likely to happen to them, the benefit of a prior visit to the home, and the skill required from staff in coping with this very crucial moment in life. The feelings of existing residents also have to be taken into account: an unknown person comes through the door displaying all the symptoms of fear and hostility, and the residents uneasily contemplate how this individual is going to affect their world and the relationships within it.

Discharge home to relatives Discharges were perceived by many as a happy outcome and the main problems were coping with the farewells and practicalities whilst attending to other residents and events in the group. Discussion in the plenary session was of a speculative nature: members wondered how they would have felt at seeing someone else going home when they could not; how the residents really felt about going to live with a relative, a step which represented yet another new phase in their life with new close relationships to cope with. Staff thought they did not have enough time to deal with discharges. Sometimes the relatives made faintly hostile comments when taking their parents away from the home and these were seen as a rejection of the care provided.

Accidents to residents For the staff the incidental accidents and crises were harassing, since they diverted their energies and attention from current matters including major events like admissions, discharges and death. To the other residents they provided a source of interest and excitement. They also released expressions of irritation or disgust, for example, when a drunken member was sick all over the floor, having succeeded in getting liquor brought in to him before lunch. Generally speaking, these events reinforced the sense of dependence on the staff, the impotence of the disabled residents and the need to mobilise by telephone at very short notice outside agencies such as the doctors, ambulance or other ancillary staff to help with lifting, undoing the clamps of the wheelchairs, etc. Yet it was acknowledged that these are very frequent occurrences in homes containing a high proportion of frail residents and should be seen as an inevitable part of the daily round.

Death of a resident In one home there was a death which had been part of the planned exercise, and in another a resident died unexpectedly. In each case the circumstances of the death and the methods of coping with the total situation within the home were a source of acute anxiety to everyone, and provoked much subsequent discussion.

In one group, the person died after a terminal illness, but staff did not directly inform other residents. It was all done by inference and dropping remarks which plainly indicated the death. This led to feelings of uncertainty during the staff member's presence in the room, followed by a hubbub when she left. 'Is it true?' 'Why don't they say outright what has happened?' This was followed fairly quickly by some argument over who was likely to inherit the single room and chair of the deceased. The removal of the bodies was another source of stress. Whilst this was universally recognised as being unavoidable, the whole approach to the subject of the death of a resident was construed as avoidance, pretending it had not happened, trying to make life go on without actually recognising that one member of the community was no longer a part of it. The staff felt considerable fear of provoking depression by too much emphasis on mortality. Staff seemed to think that residents should not be continually reminded that 'their time' might also come soon. Furthermore there was speculation that this avoidance approach might reinforce the feeling that the individual's existence hardly mattered to anyone any more.

A staff debate in one group about when the residents might be told about a death highlighted the dilemma. 'When will be the best time? Shall we tell them when they get back from their outing?' 'No, no, don't tell them then, it will spoil the day. Leave it till tomorrow'. 'We can tell them when someone asks'. In fact, nobody did ask when they all came back from the outing, and in this case the residents did not directly address any member of staff on the subject, but talked between themselves.

The later comments of the two 'deceased' were interesting. Both felt they were in some way being hidden from view, and having not actually died, they nevertheless experienced feelings of resentment that more fuss was not made about their departure from the group. The terminally ill member appreciated the fact that staff remained with her for much of the time. When she wanted to see a priest difficulties arose, but this presumably would not occur in the real life situation. What was wanted was a balance of privacy and care.

Whether or not staff should attend funerals aroused further speculation about the relationships between residents, staff and relatives.

There seemed to emerge a firm consensus that the subject of death needed far more attention in staff meetings, training and preparation for residential work.

Longer term reactions to the role-play The first response to the exercise was an intense release of feeling in the plenary session immediately afterwards. There was a high level of noise as members reassembled denoting release from the tensions of the past four hours. However, a much longer term effect continued after the actual exercise was concluded. For many participants it provided food for thought throughout the seminar and in the subsequent phases of the project.

Small group discussions contained numerous references to the events, themes and feelings provoked by the role play. It became plain as the Development Group project progressed through its various phases over the succeeding year that this had indeed been a key session in the first seminar, unlocking many doors in the mind and facilitating new approaches to change and development.

'I can't do everything for myself, but anyway they assured me the staff here don't mind'.

Getting down to work – the studies

The two studies described here are part of the fact finding which was necessary in the early stages of the project. The first section deals with the question of how dependent the elderly actually are and compares the degree of dependence experienced by elderly people in three of Brighton's residential homes with those attending one of the day centres.

The interprofessional assessment process, described next, was set up because early in the project it became clear that the way in which the elderly were assessed (usually in relation to their admission to residential care) was far from satisfactory. The assessments tended to be narrowly focussed and carried out separately by each set of workers, with little cross referencing with other workers involved in the case. Dissatisfaction with these methods gradually emerged and led to the setting up of a study into the interprofessional assessment of elderly people in Brighton.

Dependence levels – Study of thirty residents in homes for the elderly and ten clients in a day centre

The survey which follows is small and does not profess to any statistical validity, but it is nevertheless illuminating: for example residents in the three homes surveyed appeared to be more physically able than those who attended the day centre, but they were more incontinent and more mentally confused. (see Table 3 p. 48).

Substantially more medication was prescribed in residential homes than was the case in community care (Table 6). This raises the question of whether it was actually needed or whether it was convenient from the management point of view.

These and many other questions may be provoked by reading this study.

Aim and method The aim of this study, carried out in January 1977, was to give a general picture of the levels of dependence of elderly people in three residential homes and one day centre in Brighton. The last ten residents admitted to each home and every fifth person on the register of attenders at the day centre were selected as subjects. Thus ten people were selected from each establishment, giving a total sample of forty.

A form was designed by the Brighton Division of East Sussex Social Services Department to assess levels of dependence in the elderly. This form, which is reproduced at the end of this section, was completed for each member of the sample; once for the level of dependence on admission and once at the time of the survey. Forms were filled in by the officers in charge of the establishments, assisted by their residential and day care officers. The information contained in the forms was analysed using an index of dependence and a list of incapacities in terms of self-care, similar to those used in the DHSS census of residential accommodation for the elderly, carried out in East Sussex on 30 April, 1970. (1)

Index of dependence The index of dependence used had a rating scale from 3–10 points which was made up as follows:

Mobility	*Points*
1 Ambulant 2 Ambulant except stairs	1
3 Ambulant only with artificial aids 4 Ambulant only with help of others	2
5 Mobile with wheelchair	3
6 Bedfast	4
Physical Condition	
1 Continent	1
2 Only incontinent occasionally eg at night	2
3 Incontinent	3
Mental Condition	
1 Mentally alert	1
2 Mildly confused	2
3 Severely confused	3

A score of three would mean that the old person was ambulant, continent and mentally alert while a larger score would indicate that he had some problems.

Results Table 1 describes the age and sex of the sample. It will be observed that because of the different complement of the elderly in each home it is not possible statistically to compare them.

Table 1 Age and sex of sample

	Home A	Home B	Home C	Day Centre
Men, number of	5	2	2	0
average age	74 yrs	75½	76 yrs	–
Women, number of	5	8	8	10
average age	81 yrs	81	84¾	81
Men and Women average age	77½ yrs	79¾	83 yrs	81 yrs
Men and Women age range	65–89 yrs	67–93 yrs	73–91 yrs	62–88 yrs

Table 2 indicates the static nature of levels of dependence at the day centre. No change at all took place in the levels between the time of admission and the date of the survey. Change in the dependence levels in residential care was marginal, three per cent becoming more dependent and three per cent less so.

Comparison in the levels under various headings is instructive. Forty per cent in residential care were ambulant, continent and mentally alert compared with a bare ten per cent in the day centre (four times as many). Multiple problems appeared to be one cause of admission to residential care: twenty-seven per cent having multiple problems compared with less than half that number (ten per cent) at the day centre. On the contrary far more people (eighty per cent) in the day centre had only one or two problems compared with thirty-three per cent in residential care.

Table 2 Percentage of elderly people having particular indices of dependence

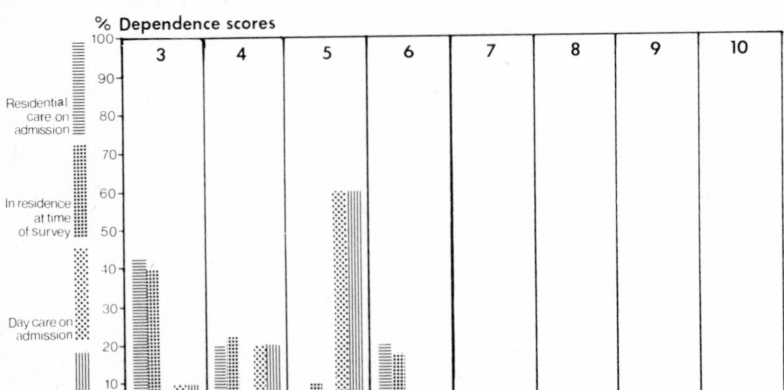

A pen picture begins to emerge (see Table 3) of the occupants of the three homes and the day centre in Brighton. The people in the day centre were less ambulant than those in residence (except that there were three bedfast residents in the homes), and there was a preponderance of wheelchair users in the day centre (sixty per cent compared with three per cent in the homes). Mental confusion and some degree of incontinence seemed to be two of the important factors which could lead to admission to these residential homes.

Table 3 Breakdown of the indices of dependence at the time of the survey

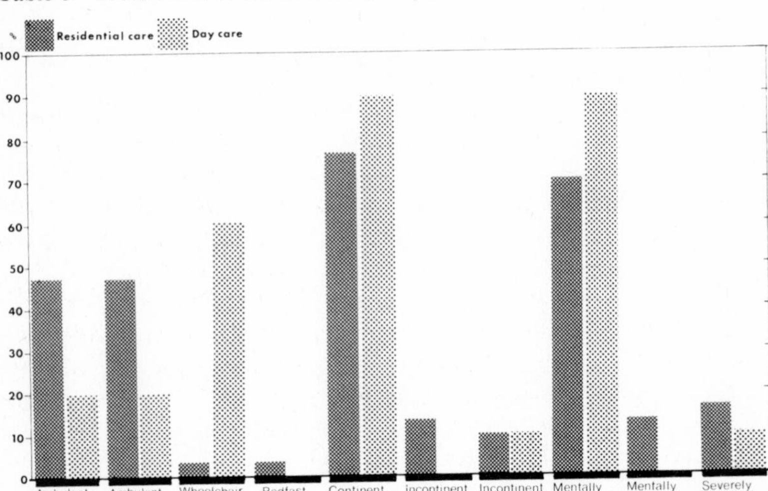

Incapacities in terms of self care The number of incapacities in terms of self care were assessed using a list of incapacities as follows:
Unable to feed unaided
Unable to dress unaided
Unable to wash unaided
Unable to bath unaided
Unable to use toilet unaided
The list of five gave a rating scale of 0 to 5, 0 signifying that no assistance was needed for any of the above and, at the other extreme, 5 signifying that assistance was necessary for all of them.

The changes in abilities were again marginal (as Table 4 shows). In residential care three per cent had slightly improved since admission, whilst six per cent had deteriorated and at the time of the survey had a higher number of incapacities. Twenty per cent of day care attenders on the other hand had deteriorated slightly.

Table 4 Percentage of elderly people having a number of incapacities

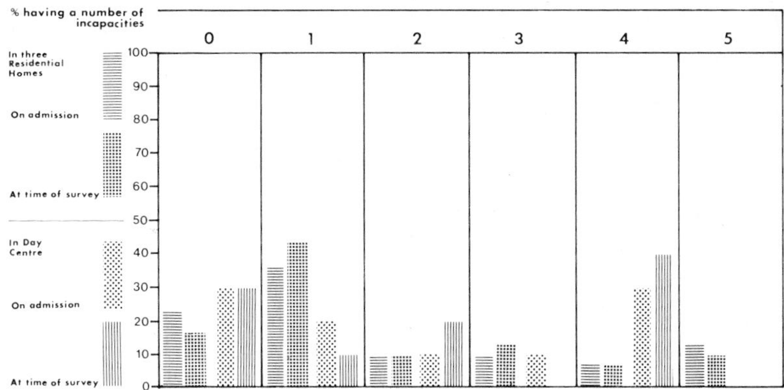

Table 5 particularises the changes according to incapacity. The deterioration since admission was just over twice as high in the day centre (thirty per cent as against fourteen). This deterioration was particularly related to the ability to wash and dress and use the toilet unaided: all vital elements if someone is to remain in the community. Improvement occurred in residential care in relation to the ability to wash, dress and bath unaided.

Table 5 Percentage of elderly people having particular incapacities

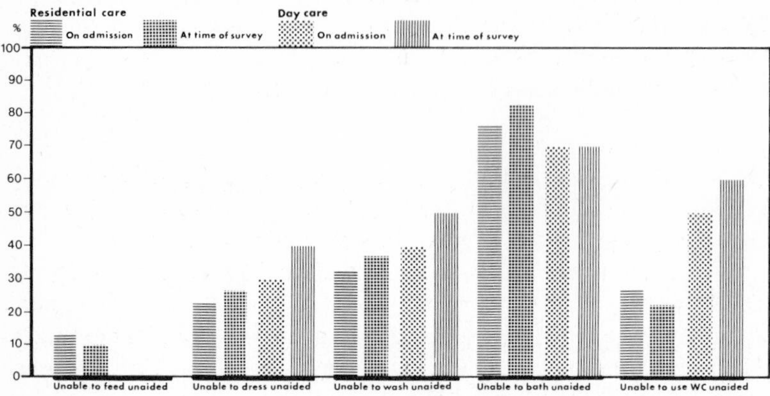

Medical prescribing The level of regular medication at the time of the survey was twenty seven per cent higher in residential homes than in the day centre. (see Table 6). Forty per cent of those in the day centre received only occasional medication or none, compared with thirteen per cent in the residential homes.

Table 6 Percentage of elderly people receiving medication

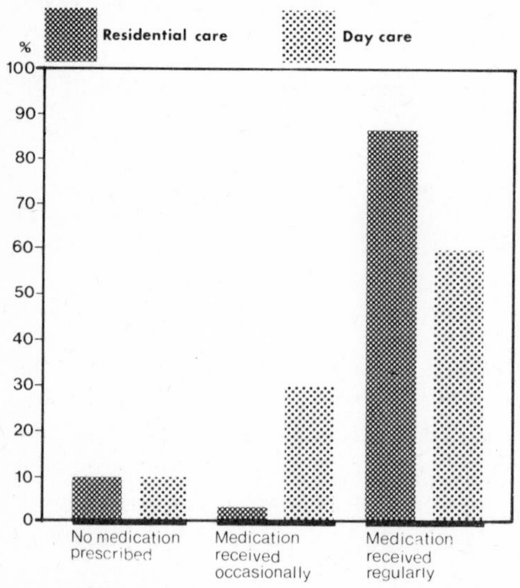

Conclusions Combining the conclusions from the tables on indices of dependence, incapacities in terms of self care and medical needs, and using the figures at the time of the survey, a general picture of the elderly people in the day centre as compared with those in the three residential homes emerges, and is shown in Table 7.

Table 7 Percentage of elderly people having particular capacities at the time of the survey

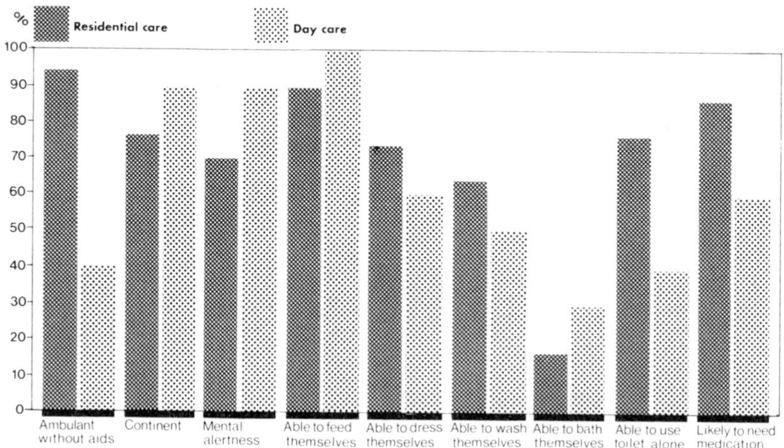

FORM USED TO GATHER DATA ON DEPENDENCE LEVELS

HOME		DATE	CASE NO
RESIDENT'S NAME			SOCIAL WORKER
SEX	DATE OF BIRTH	AGE	DATE OF ADMISSION
MEDICAL DETAILS:		PROGNOSIS: Stable/Improve Deterioration	

DETAILS OF RESIDENT	DEGREE OF INCAPACITY AMOUNT OF ASSISTANCE	NONE NEVER	SLIGHT RARELY	MODERATE OCCASION-ALLY	COM-PLETE FRE-QUENTLY
1. MOBILITY Does the resident require assistance to: i. Walk? Aid.Wheelchair.Attendant ii. Climb stairs? iii. Is resident bedfast?					
2. SELF CARE Does the resident require assistance to: i. Feed? ii. Dress or undress? iii. Wash face and hands? iv. Bath? v. Shave? vi. Use the toilet?					
3. PHYSICAL CONDITION i. Is this resident incontinent? Day/Night ii. Does this resident require surgical dressings? iii. Does this resident require medication ie drugs or injections? iv. Does this resident require a special diet?					
4. MENTAL CONDITION Does this resident exhibit i. Anti-social or self harming behaviour ie needs close or constant supervision? ii. Confusion ie does not readily understand request, or has poor orientation of place and people? iii. Is the resident mentally alert ?) mildly confused ?) Delete N/A severely confused?)					
TOTAL					

Inter-professional assessment – A pilot study

The term 'interprofessional assessment' was used locally to describe this piece of work, although 'multi-service' assessment might be a more accurate term. One of the working parties set up following the first seminar of the Development Group project, which comprised representatives of a variety of disciplines including residential workers, home help organisers, nursing officers, social workers and voluntary workers, suggested that a pilot scheme for interprofessional assessment should be established. The management team of Brighton Division of East Sussex Social Services Department accepted this proposal.

Previous methods of assessment Referrals were normally handled in the Division either by social workers or the home help section. The intake workers had the responsibility of assessing the situation and offering appropriate help immediately or in the short term. If long term help or support were required the situation was reviewed and transferred to a social worker in one of the long term teams.

Terms of reference for the project The pilot scheme started on 17 October 1977 and was set up to run for three months or one hundred referrals, whichever was the shorter. During the period there was a shortage of referrals from this area and only fifty-one cases were assessed by the panel. The referrals came from a circumscribed area of Brighton, and those judged inappropriate to the social services department by the intake team were excluded. The aim was to get a good cross section of cases during the pilot period.

Description of the area The area chosen for the survey was a small section of the north-west part of the town, covering two square miles. It was a hilly part of old Brighton containing Victorian and early twentieth century housing, with small blocks of modern development.

There was little council accommodation and most of the housing was terraced, with few blocks of flats. Many people referred to the project lived in multi-occupied older dwellings. There were five doctors' surgeries, although several other doctors also served the area. Six post offices were located in the area but four were on the extremities and only two were central.

Many of those in the survey had lived in the area for twenty years or more and experienced quite a lot of support from others living in the same district. On the other hand there were complaints about the problems arising from the changing nature of this part of Brighton. The arrival of a polytechnic and a university had led to an increase in the demand for rented accommodation at a time when such accommodation was in any case becoming less available. Tensions between young and elderly tenants in multi-occupied houses and terraced housing soon came to light and redevelopment, leading to increased rents and consequent pressure upon elderly tenants to leave, was also a problem.

The entire area was within ten to fifteen minutes' walk of the station. This had artificially raised rents and house values, as had the fact that the area was in a central position close to the main shopping centre and places of entertainment.

There was no warden controlled or sheltered accommodation in the district and only one residential establishment, along with one day centre run by the Red Cross.

The panel The joint assessment panel met every week and comprised the following:

(a) Intake social workers, or social services officers, as appropriate.
(b) Home help organiser
(c) Community nursing officer, representing the health visitors and community nurses working in the area
(d) Representative of the housing department
(e) Representative of the hospital social work team.

The panel was chaired by an intake social worker, and a member of the Development Group attended as an observer to monitor the project.

The chairman of the panel and the home help organiser lived in the sample area and were able to bring a great deal of local knowledge to panel meetings. The home help organiser was a member of the local community association and she also assisted her husband in his shop.

The objectives of interprofessional assessment

(a) To match the provision of services to the assessed needs of individual clients;
(b) to enable the resources of all agencies to be deployed in the most effective way;

(c) to develop effective liaison between agencies and a better understanding of the approaches different agencies have to individual needs;
(d) to improve communications between agencies and to record more accurate information;
(e) to use this information to ease transfers between workers and from community to residential and hospital care, and to assist in reviews etc;
(f) to identify areas of unmet need which may lead to the development of new services or the recognition of existing services.

Records A record of clients included in the project was kept by the intake team clerk. In order to avoid any duplication and double visiting these included clients referred through the home help service. The assessment form, which is reproduced at the end of this section, had previously been used in a similar experiment in the Eastbourne Division of East Sussex Social Services Department.

Method As soon as a referral was identified a note was sent to all members of the panel. This gave outline details of the case and named the social worker or home help organiser responsible for completing the forms. By this means members of the panel were notified of clients who would be assessed at the next meeting. Each member was then expected to search for relevant information he might have about the client which could help a joint assessment. In addition they discussed the situation with their colleagues, checked records and read the appropriate notes. They were not, however, expected to visit the client. Instead an intake worker or home help organiser, as appropriate, visited, completed the assessment form and presented the case to the panel.

In the course of the project the home help organiser completed twenty-six visits, intake social workers or trainees seven, and intake social services officers twenty.

Results There were fifty-one referrals, involving fifty-six individuals. Five of these were married couples and, of the single persons, ten were male and thirty-six female. A married couple is counted as one referral.

Table 1 reason for referral (as stated by referee)

Home help	26
Social work help and advice	8
Part III long or short stay	8
Day care	2
Aids, telephone etc	3
At risk	6
TOTAL	53 (2 clients referred for more than one service)

(*Note* Although home help was requested in 26 cases, only 13 of the clients were unknown to the home help organiser.)

Table 2 Source of referral

	Referrals
Health Service	
Health visitor	12
General practitioner	2
District nurse	1
Hospitals: social worker	6
medical	3
Ambulance control	1
Family, friends, general public, anonymous	15
Referrals from social services department	3
Other agencies	8
TOTAL	51

Table 3 Sex and age of referrals

	M	F	Totals
90 years and over	2	5	7
80–99 years	6	21	27
70–79 years	3	11	14
60–69 years	4	3	8

Table 4 How the cases were dealt with

Several people were referred to more than one agency so that figures below exceed the actual cases.

Home help provided*	11
To voluntary agencies	8
To housing department	5
To health departments†	3
Aids provided	3
Social work support	3
Cases closed after advice	7
Cases closed as inappropriate‡	7
or refusal to co-operate	3

*Reasons for the discrepancy between the 26 requests for home help and the 11 allocated are as follows:—

Pending	2	
Inappropriate	2	
Refused	8	
Admitted to hospital	1	
Private help obtained	2	(cheaper)
Rehoused	1	

† Many clients were already supported by the health services before referral to the panel.

‡ Examples of these would be the neighbour who referred for home help when client already had private help.

Evaluation The panel met regularly, attendance was high and a good level of discussion was sustained. However, there were times when the members felt they had failed to think broadly enough or to explore the needs of the client fully.

The discrepancy in the panel's levels of representation caused some problems. Whilst the area social worker who presented the case was the one who had actually visited the client it was not possible to ensure that this was the case with the other members. The hospital social work team for instance was represented by only one of its members and the health visitors and community nurses by a community nursing officer. In the case of the housing department, however, the fact that the representative was the principal assistant (management) did not make for difficulties as he was inevitably closely involved with the situations discussed in the panel. It was thought that having hospital social workers and nurses who were likewise fully and personally informed on the cases under discussion would have made for a higher level of discussion.

Of the fifty-one cases referred to the panel twenty-seven were judged to have gained significantly from a joint assessment. Six cases were subject to review and sixteen were inappropriate referrals. One was closed after the first visit.

The following are some examples of what were considered to be 'gains':

Improved co-ordination An eighty-five year old client was referred to the home help organiser by her GP for help pending her admission to hospital for possible terminal care. During the panel discussion it transpired that the health visitor was not aware of the situation. Following the discussion she and the hospital social worker were briefed about the client's background so that she could more easily help after admission. Agencies were thus alerted to the present situation and warned of complications should the situation deteriorate. The client's wish not to have strangers around her at the moment was at the same time respected.

Better use of resources At a more practical level knowledge about a whole range of community facilities was shared for the first time. A referral for help with moving house for instance led to an exchange of information about the most appropriate removal firm. Different approaches to the problems were shared at panel meetings and the problems of the various agencies were better appreciated.

Anticipation of problems An important development was that the panel came to be in a position to foresee potential problem areas and areas of unmet need. This led on to their devising new ways of meeting need. One specific instance was when the housing department embarked on a three year programme of rehousing. It was soon realised by the assessment panel that there would be a need for social work support for many tenants during preparation for the move itself and this and subsequent resettlement were fully discussed. This was important because, as the pattern of tenancy changed, elderly people were often left in isolated and vulnerable situations. On another occasion presentation of a case led to a general discussion on transport needs and the possibility of establishing a luncheon club to cater for a specific area.

Improved analysis of the problem In fifteen cases the joint analysis of the problem led to a realisation that cross referrals should be made, to other agencies or to different parts of the same agency. On one occasion a client referred by the consultant physician for domiciliary services (although already in receipt of home help) was also referred by the panel to the housing department and the health visitor. On another occasion the reverse process operated. A visit by the home help organiser led to a client being referred to the geriatric health visitor with a view to a full medical assessment.

Other points arising from the evaluation were:

Assessment form The elderly needs assessment form was found to be a useful basic tool for gathering information, and copies were exchanged between agencies. The form was adapted by the housing department for use in housing assessment, particularly for elderly or handicapped persons. Whilst it was not always necessary or desirable to complete the whole form more information was put on files when the forms were used which would be of considerable help in future allocation, assessment or review meetings.

Admission to residential care There was an exceptionally low referral rate for residential care. Only seven clients were referred on this account. No long term care was arranged and in only one case was this type of care necessary at all, and that was on a short term basis. Of the seven clients referred one was admitted to hospital, one refused to consider residential care and the remaining five clients had their needs met in other ways. It was impossible to say whether this low referral pattern was by chance or perhaps because the field workers' approach to problems had changed so that they no longer saw residential care as the only obvious solution.

Conclusions

General The panel was successful in developing understanding, improving communications and recording and using this information to ease transfers. Several areas of unmet need were identified and improvements were made in enabling the resources of all agencies to be deployed in the most effective way. There was also considerable movement in matching the provision of services to the assessed needs of individual clients.

The future If the interprofessional assessment scheme were to be adopted on a more general basis there would be a need for a series of short training sessions for all workers involved. This should include a survey of the neighbourhood, its amenities, facilities and geography.

If training were available it should be possible to extend the interprofessional aspects of assessment. The panel could receive referrals, nominate a 'key worker' who would visit, complete the forms and then request information from all other agencies involved. The panel would then decide, on the strength of the collated evidence and subsequent discussion, the most appropriate form of intervention. The scheme could be further extended by including representatives from residential care, social security and voluntary organisations.

Resources Should this scheme be extended considerably further resources would be necessary. It would, therefore, be unrealistic to recommend the general extension of the scheme for all referrals of the elderly. The panel worked well within the constraints mentioned and also because of the character and administrative convenience of the chosen area. This experience could be built upon if a way could be found to 'screen' the cases referred to the panel.

Confidentiality The issue of confidentiality was constantly in the panel's mind during this pilot scheme but no significant problems were encountered.

Reference

[1]Key Issue 1, The Elderly, Summary of Findings, 1976. Available from East Sussex County Council Social Services Department.

INTERPROFESSIONAL ASSESSMENT OF ELDERLY CLIENTS
(PILOT PROJECT)

PART I

CHECK LIST

NAME OF CLIENT ....

HOUSING - Council/Private Rented/Owner Occupied/Other*

(i) Is the client potentially homeless? YES/NO* If YES details ......

....

(ii) Is the client living alone? YES/NO* If NO with whom is he living?

NAME	Approx Age	Relationship To Client	When present eg all day, part-day, all night, part night, all time.

(iii) Is the client's accommodation suitable? YES/NO* If NO please state why (eg poor access, stairs, toilet arrangements) ....

....

(iv) Other important areas of concern on housing (eg heating, state of cleanliness, cooking facilities, safety etc) ....

....

....

(v) How long has client lived in present home? immediate area?

FINANCIAL NEED

(i) Would client be able to afford private services, if available? YES/NO*

(ii) Does client's income appear to be sufficient to provide warmth, food, clothing, etc? YES/NO*

(iii) Is client aware of the appropriate welfare rights? YES/NO*

‘They told me there’d always be someone to look after me, because that’s what I was worried about’.

The workers – their views

It has been more difficult to provide readers with an idea about the views of the workers involved in the project than to represent those of the elderly people interviewed at the beginning of the exercise. The group of elderly interviewees were limited in number and their views circumscribed by the nature of the interviews carried out with them. The workers on the other hand were many and various, being drawn mainly from all levels of social services, health care and voluntary organisations, with different backgrounds and experiences.

Participants had had the opportunity to read articles circulated beforehand containing current thinking, and many of the ideas were not new to them, but in this chapter the beginnings of changes in attitude can be perceived. Workers can be seen coming to terms with the effects of any new stance they may decide to take up in their work and what it will mean to themselves, their colleagues and most of all to their clients.

The views expressed here are drawn from three separate events. The first section is concerned with the seminar held in Brighton in April 1977. Following that event three working groups were established to examine different areas of policy and practice. A selection of the points arising from these groups has been provided next. The last section deals with the events of the second seminar held in February 1978.

Exploring the principles [the first seminar, April 1977]

The members of the first seminar had been confronted with a great deal of material. In addition to the presentation of papers from visiting speakers there had been a video tape of interviews with clients or residents and a role playing exercise. There was much to assimilate and in essence, at this seminar, all were concerned to thrash out the principles on which the care of elderly people in Brighton should be based and to discover more clearly where they, as individuals, now stood in response to this. Risk taking, for instance, is a fundamental issue, particularly in relation to residential care, but it is also integral to all other forms of care for the elderly. The comments on this subject are therefore placed first and followed by those which derive from it.

Risk-taking The responsibility for allowing residents to take risks or 'live dangerously' should, it was thought, be shared amongst staff at all levels. Whilst the basic idea was that everyone should be allowed to attempt the fullest possible range of activities, having regard to their total condition, it was realised that, on occasions, residents might be attempting things beyond their physical or mental capacities. It was thought possible that the application of the new ideas might prove dangerous for some residents and, should things go badly wrong staff feared they would be in the direct firing line of any public protest. It was extremely important, therefore, that all levels of staff should feel adequately supported when any new regime was introduced.

There was seen to be a special need for understanding and support from the health services, including general practitioners. This was particularly important in situations where residents were responsible for their own medication. At present general practitioners were likely to see residential homes as protective, rather than supportive of independent life and they were, therefore, likely to act in accordance with this belief.

The following matters were explored in respect of risk-taking:

residents taking baths alone;

residents making hot drinks and snacks, involving the use of electrical appliances and boiling water;

residents ironing and cleaning which involved bending down;

a range of more varied activities within the grounds and the home itself;

the use of voluntary workers, eg taking frail people out;

residents being alone in their bedrooms for a significant period of time, eg during personal washing, when they might fall and injure themselves;

the locking of room doors;

the question of insurance for loss and damage of residents' belongings. No one appeared to know who would be responsible, nor whether insurance could be claimed.

Home helps All agreed that the home help service had received a great deal of attention in some respects, whilst it was almost taken for granted in others. It seemed to be assumed that this service, whatever its constraints, must be the main instrument for keeping clients in the community. Too often it was taken for granted that home helps would offer a wide range of support and assistance, sometimes beyond the call of duty. Many became friends of the household and performed voluntary tasks which would otherwise fall upon either the department or other agencies.

Although there was some demand that this should be a service on which cuts fell last in times of economy there was little evidence that the service of a home help kept clients at home who would otherwise be in residential care. There was a suggestion that a project focussed on this point might enhance the standing of the home help service.

The home help recording system and their integration more fully into the social services department as a whole were also thorny problems. It seemed to members that, at present, the section largely functioned as a separate entity, and because their records were kept separately it was often hard for other workers to retrieve them. In addition insufficient regard was paid to the mine of information individual home helps had available. Home helps themselves would also benefit from receiving information from others working with clients.

The question of a modern role for the home help was thrashed out. She should, it was thought, be a key person in the rehabilitative process. Indeed the attitudes of home helps could do much to encourage either dependence or continued activity in their clients. Even a small amount of encouragement to the client to do odd jobs in the house (as a supplement to the activities of the home help) might prevent the deterioration of an elderly person. It was considered that a home help should no longer be regarded basically as a domestic cleaner but as someone whose methods could play an important part in shaping the client's life. Conditions of service obviously had to be laid out in legal terms but it should be possible to explore methods of lifting some of the petty restrictions on what they could 'officially' undertake and this, in itself, would help in clarifying their new role.

The financing of the home help service was also discussed and the point made that it was now possible for someone on a high assessment to obtain private domestic help more cheaply. Might not the social services department or the voluntary agencies offer to mobilise private help if this was wanted? The goal in all cases should surely be to find the most appropriate solution to the client's circumstances and needs, whether this was on a public or a private basis.

Day care Day care was seen as another alternative to full-time residential care. There was, however, much debate about the form this should take. More day care should be provided in the opinion of most but there was considerable confusion as to how this might best come about. Much discussion took place about the desirability of having day visitors intruding into the homes of long term residents. As well as the problems in human relationships created by having outsiders coming into the homes such visitors also introduced new ideas and a change of atmosphere which could make the whole scene much more interesting.

The practicalities of having additional people coming into the homes had to be carefully weighed. There must be sufficient chairs, enough space and a welcoming atmosphere in the dining room and elsewhere in the home. Transport was always a problem. Day care clients often had long journeys and ambulances were late in collecting them. Consequently they sometimes arrived tired and harassed and all too quickly had to get ready to start the return trip. In these circumstances any personal care such as bathing, hair washing and chiropody had to be crammed into a short space of time and became a hasty process. All too readily what should be an enjoyable day out became an irritation and perhaps something of a nightmare.

Casework with the elderly Whether or not there was a need for social workers to undertake casework with elderly clients was debated at some length. Historical influences were thought by one member to have played some part in the present situation in which the elderly were given only low priority for casework services from social workers.

Although the attachment of social workers to general practitioners had brought about some deeper involvement on the part of social workers, East Sussex undoubtedly appeared to afford higher priority to fieldwork with other client groups, such as children, whose needs were perceived as more urgent. If, however, fieldworkers were going to undertake more thorough-going work with elderly clients their 'servicing' by the administration needed to be a great deal more efficient than it was at present.

The question of record keeping and of passing information from one branch of the service to another was a troublesome one. Just as it was important for social workers visiting potential residents to have adequate information, so also were the residential staff very dependent upon social workers for information about the background and social circumstances of clients. Current practice varied considerably. Sometimes records were received before the client, but in many

cases they arrived much later. Discussion of these issues raised many others such as:
should clients' records be kept in the homes?
who should have access to the records?
should some aspects be kept confidential to certain members of staff only?
what continuing use should be made of the elderly needs assessment form?

Continuity of casework was seen to be important but how was it to be achieved? Were field and residential staff to become interchangeable? Was it, for instance, essential that fieldworkers carried out the assessment visits? Why not a member of the residential team? The home help, indeed, might be the person with the most important contribution to make, because she had had a daily encounter with the client in their own home and therefore had detailed knowledge of their capacities.

Out of this discussion arose the concept of the 'key worker'. If the 'key worker' idea could be tried out it should be possible for each group to support the others through difficult or unfamiliar situations without one of them necessarily assuming prime responsibility. This was seen as an exciting development for the future.

Admissions to residential care Much time in the groups was devoted to the question of admissions procedure. Everyone recognised that this was a particularly traumatic period for the elderly person and that both residents and staff needed time to make it as welcoming and easy as possible. Adequate information about the homes was extremely important for any prospective resident and one group felt so strongly about this that they produced a draft prospectus for a fictitious home. It was not, they demonstrated, a difficult or time-consuming exercise, therefore it should be regarded as a basic necessity, so that nobody should be expected to enter an establishment about which they had no information apart from a minimal verbal description.

A particularly strong recommendation from the groups was that officers in charge of homes should visit residents before admission.

Residential living This subject occupied a great deal of time in the discussion groups, and the results of their deliberations have been collected under various headings.

Residents' rooms Privacy and a territory to call one's own were seen as the important elements associated with residents' rooms. A small, but vital, point in this connection was the question of knocking on residents' doors before entry. Too often staff walked in unannounced, thus demonstrating their lack of respect for the privacy of the person concerned. Labels with the occupant's name on it were rarely to be found on the doors of residents' rooms, but to provide them could help their sense of belonging.

The pattern of the day Times of rising, of meals and of going to bed dominate the day's activities for a resident – in complete contrast to the style of life most had had before they were admitted to care. In their own homes (although limited perhaps by circumstances and disabilities) they were able to choose the way they ordered each day. All this changed, it was thought, once the institutional regime in a home for the elderly took over. Now elderly people were liable to be treated as objects and expected to comply and adapt themselves to a set pattern, however painfully.

This set pattern of the day had its roots in long-standing patterns of work for day and night staff and these resulted all too often in residents being roused in the early hours of the morning and 'put to bed', like children, early in the evening. Presentations by visiting speakers had, however, demonstrated that this pattern was by no means inescapable. It was quite possible to be flexible about the time of rising and to permit residents to retire whenever they wished or whenever was appropriate to their physical and mental condition.

Members thought that some staff groups might oppose any change in the pattern of life because it would affect the routines of work to which they had become accustomed. It was stressed that in the process of development it was often more difficult to change the attitudes of staff than of residents. A simple illustration of this related to bedmaking. In many homes it was expected that beds would be made by a certain time in the morning, but there seemed no reason why some residents should not make their own beds in their own time. In some homes there were prohibitions against having a rest or a 'lie down' when the residents felt they needed to, which seemed indefensible.

Meals Can mealtimes be flexible, a choice of menu offered and self-catering facilities provided? Argument around these questions formed a major part of this debate and it was not universally accepted that all these things could be provided.

The subject appeared ready for a major overhaul. One set time for a mass meal was seen as undesirable and various alternatives were put forward. A flexible meal service was one possibility, and this could be easier to introduce when small living groups had been established. Light meals such as breakfast or afternoon tea could also be prepared by some residents for themselves.

The time of the final meal of the day was a matter for concern. It seemed that too often high tea was in the early evening with no hot drink later in the evening, so that residents had to endure a long period of fasting each day. Residents should be consulted about menus and more choice should be provided if possible. Budgets limited the choices, but the stimulus to provide more varied fare would undoubtedly find a response in the catering staff if they could be involved in the problem. In this connection, however, the bulk puchase of provisions on contract was raised by the senior staff of some homes, who found that this method prevented them from achieving a reasonable variety of foodstuffs. The method was undoubtedly economical, but its effects upon the standards of catering in the homes must be questioned.

Furniture and furnishings As yet, there were insufficient opportunities for people to bring some of their own furniture or other possessions into homes. More lockable cupboards, drawers and cabinets were needed and it was questioned why it often proved so difficult to organise locks in residential establishments: the cost could not be so excessive.

Residents should use their own personal incomes to buy radios and portable televisions so that each resident might lead a more independent life. It was pointed out that this practice was commonplace in many homes provided by voluntary organisations who did not expect to provide expensive furniture except to supplement residents' property.

The role play had raised the question about residents being consulted on the design and decoration of the homes. No doubt such matters as colour schemes and furnishings would cause much disagreement, but at least the residents could be asked for their views. Neutral colours and soft furnishings might be the best solution for residents' rooms as a background for their own possessions.

Activities in the home There were many illustrations of the ways in which varied activities could be introduced to make life more interesting. The grounds surrounding the homes were often very under-used. Many residents had left a much-loved garden, and some of the men had been used to spending a good part of their day gardening. Expert help could be obtained to enable the residents to continue this central activity of their lives. For many years the DHSS has funded a project to develop methods of gardening for the elderly and handicapped, and literature was available on the subject. In one home some residents had part-time paid occupations, for example dressmaking, and others had a variety of skills which could be developed further.

Medical care The question of medical care in the homes and the use by residents of the health service facilities provided for the community was a subject which deserved further examination. Some of the issues raised in this connection were:
a resident's right to keep his own GP;
privacy when consulting the doctor;
decisions about the capacity of residents to administer their own medication;
a home nursing service for residents;
retention of rooms during admission to hospital;
care of terminally ill residents;
follow-up by hospital social workers, if this would help residents in the transition to the new home.

Finance There was general agreement that this was a complex and delicate subject; Some of the reasons for this were:
i. The public often thought social services departments only provided for people who were unable to afford private accommodation.
ii. Residents who found that when assessed they had to pay the full fees often expressed bitterness and anger, especially when they saw others from similar walks of life in the same home paying less because they had been less thrifty in providing for their old age. On this basis, it was agreed that where residents had adequate capital they should have the option of entering a private home.
iii Prospective residents should be given written information, supplemented by verbal explanation, about the method of assessment, what they would have to pay and what the process of assessment involved.
iv. It was recognised that many members of the older generation resented divulging their financial affairs. In addition the complicated assessment process often made it difficult to tell applicants the rate of

contribution before admission. Nevertheless, it was felt that serious attention must be given to the assessment process as it provoked so much bad feeling. Workers themselves felt they would not enter into a long term commitment without having enough prudence to assess beforehand what it would cost, and this highlighted the way in which the system treated clients impersonally.

v. It was felt that there should be a county policy about the handling of pension books, as staff felt uneasy about removing residents' books. This caused resentment as many residents were able to handle their own affairs.

iv. Residents should be encouraged to spend their money on ordinary necessities and luxuries such as clothing, TV sets, radios and continental quilts.

vii. There was a request that systems of handling money and charging for residents in private homes should be looked at more carefully. These clients might be even more vulnerable because they were removed from the public system.

viii. Importance was attached to the manner in which personal allowances were dispensed. Some homes appeared to do this as a sort of public 'pay parade', which insulted residents' dignity.

Communication Staff at 'grass roots' level lacked effective means of communication, and they wanted to know who made decisions to start the processes of change. Did the prime responsibility for such decisions lie with management or with basic grade staff? By what means could residential staff make their views known to the officer in charge without appearing to be critical? It was concluded that ideally initiatives should come from each residential unit and its staff.

Achieving change Only if residents, staff, middle management and fieldworkers worked together to promote agreed goals would there be any sense of purposeful activity towards change. Could management staff be free-ranging and constructive in their approach? It was commented that everything that had been considered had been said before, but had not been acted upon or put to the test constructively.

Integration There was little point in talking about ways of assisting social services, health services and voluntary bodies to work more closely and fruitfully together until the social services department had put its own house in order. The basic need was for improved internal communication.

The working groups [summer 1977]

Discussions carried out by working groups, established for a specific purpose and meeting regularly over a set period of time, tend to have a different flavour from those which take place in the groups coming together at seminars. This was the case with the deliberations of the three working groups established after the first seminar in the project and is reflected in the following pages. The groups' remit was to examine different facets of policy and practice and to make recommendations. Some of the points made were new to Brighton division, to the department as a whole and to the care of the elderly in general, but others were recapitulations of earlier policies, both local and national.

Many different workers took part in these groups – between eighty and a hundred in all. They were taken from all sections of the social services department, home helps, home help and home care organisers, social workers and their senior officers, residential and day care officers and their co-ordinator, residential workers in homes for the elderly, at all levels of the hierarchy; workers in day centres, training and development officers, community workers; a principal assistant from the housing department, workers in voluntary organisations; health services workers, including community nurses and nursing officers, community physicians, geriatricians; and Social Work Service Officers from DHSS Development Group and Social Work Service Southern Region. The groups met fortnightly over a three month period and, in that time, managed to cover a great deal of ground. In the main their concern was directed at the organisation and structure of the services Brighton provides for its elderly people and a considerable number of positive suggestions for changing these were made.

The working groups' reports proved to be a goldmine of information and thinking. The selected summary of the points made which is provided here may, inevitably, appear somewhat staccato in nature, but it is hoped it will provide some idea of the working groups' efforts. No reference is made to the individual groups from which the comments derive. The complete summary of the working groups' thinking can be found on pages 86/117 of Volume I and the full reports in Volume II of Patterns of Care for the Elderly.

The comments have been roughly grouped under headings. However, one key point transcends these groupings and is made first.

Priority work The department should give consideration to making a policy statement on the value and priority of work with the elderly.

Community care Consideration should be given to the extent to which the elderly themselves can take part in planning and providing day care services.

Home helps A good deal could be done to achieve a wider use of home helps and this should be explored. The development role of the home care organiser should be examined. Computerisation of time sheets and other administrative tasks of home help organisers should be considered.

The effects of increased charges for the home help service should be considered.

Day centres Extra vehicles and drivers should be provided for day centre use.

Consideration should be given to a proposal that some voluntary organisations might raise funds to purchase a minibus, to be shared amongst a number of residential homes.

Discussions should take place between housing department, social services and the voluntary sector to encourage day care visitors to use common rooms in sheltered housing accommodation.

Attention should be paid to the location of existing day facilities, including luncheon clubs, so that gaps may be filled and resources brought within reach of as many elderly people as possible.

All extensions of day care facilities should be the subject of joint discussions between representatives of health and social services authorities and appropriate voluntary organisations.

There should be continuing discussions between the voluntary organisations and health and social services to ensure that the new day centre to be funded by Brighton Age Concern and built near the town centre was planned in the best way to meet local need.

Inter-disciplinary working and communication Consideration should be given to the following areas of overlap between health and social services:

i. the role of the geriatric health visitor/auxiliary vis-a-vis the social worker in supportive visiting;

ii. diagnosis of medical need in respect of home help applicants;

iii. relative duties of home helps and district nurses visiting the same clients;

iv. provision of aids.

Whilst acknowledging that some discussion to improve liaison would be an advantage, to lay too much stress on defining precisely who did what could be detrimental to the services given, where a degree of flexibility was essential.

Methods needed to be developed to increase communication, particularly in identifying the number of workers involved in a case. A 'visiting liaison card', to be agreed between all agencies, on which visitors would record dates of visits and any information a further visitor should have, should be introduced. Communications between social services and health services could be improved and the following means were suggested:

i. Meetings of appropriate staff in social work teams with appropriate health visitors and community nursing teams.

ii. Mutual distribution of organisation charts of social services and the health district (who does what).

Working relationships between social services and health district personnel should be reviewed in the light of overlapping boundaries. There was inadequate understanding of each others' policies, objectives and criteria, particularly at operational level.

Suggestions for resolving this included:

i. Structured collaborative discussions between the social services department division and the housing department about the development of common policies.

ii. Joint assessment by housing, health and social services for residential accommodation and for sheltered housing.

iii. Age Concern to be involved at an early stage in any implementation of these suggestions.

iv. Better liaison at all levels to be established. Meetings between the social services department divisional director, social services managers and senior housing management staff should take place more regularly, and there should be stronger links between social services officers and wardens of sheltered housing.

Attention should be given to the establishment of effective channels of communication between statutory and voluntary agencies.

Further work needed to be done to consider the integration of hospital social workers into the social services department, in particular the need to look at what hospital social worker teams had in common with intake teams and the way this approach to their work could be developed.

It was considered important that the pilot study at present under way in the Brighton Health District to study the integration of hospital social workers' records into the social services department's recording system should be pursued. In the transfer of cases from hospital to divisions a good hospital work summary was needed as well as general information.

Hospital social workers should be included in meetings with team leaders and social workers.

The attendance of a home help organiser at hospital discharge meetings should be extended where appropriate.

Assessment and admissions to residential care Admissions should be carefully planned. All clients should be visited by the officer in charge, preferably jointly with the fieldworker, and residents should have a chance to visit the home. The fieldworker should keep the case open until the first review, which he should attend. The social worker and the officer in charge should decide who was the key worker with the client and his family, and that person should be accountable for the case.

Officers in charge should attend allocation meetings. The presentation of cases at allocation meetings and the process of admission to care should be improved.

Consideration should be given to the setting up of a small emergency admissions unit for the elderly.

The hospital 'swap system' should be abolished.

Consideration should be given to the problems relating to the referral of clients by hospital social workers for divisional resources.

Further consideration should be given to the setting up of a panel consisting of representatives of housing, health and social services to discuss referrals for sheltered housing and to consider allocations and transfers.

There was still a long way to go in the development of common policies, attitudes and aims which would lead to agreed criteria for sheltered housing, health and social services care. The adoption of a joint health and social services elderly needs assessment process, with some input from housing would be a big step forward.

A pilot multidisciplinary assessment scheme should be implemented.

Assessment should take place during the early part of a stay in residential care, and should form part of the ongoing review process.

Residential care Admission to residential care should not deprive any individual of any rights of access to community resources.

Consideration should be given to increasing the provision of short stay places as a preventive measure and also as a means of reassuring potential residents about the benefit of residential care.

The use of rotating care should be extended in appropriate cases to maintain the client as long as possible in the community. In such cases agreement should be reached between client, relatives and social services department about their respective obligations and responsibilities.

The officer in charge should have discretion about the use of staff hours, and there should be an overlap of time between shifts to facilitate continuity of care, particularly for night staff.

More flexibility should be allowed in early morning and evening routines, and the practice of night staff waking residents very early should cease.

The practice of routine bathing should cease, and where residents desire privacy and are capable of bathing themselves without undue risk supervision should not be exercised.

Some occupational therapy should be available to all homes.

A public telephone should be available in each home.

A policy should be established about the distribution of funeral flowers, and relatives and the general public should be informed about gifts to the home in lieu of flowers.

Consideration should be given to helping staff in their approach to the care of dying residents.

A formal review of each resident should take place between six weeks and three months after admission and regularly thereafter, not less than annually. Residents should be involved in their reviews, together with their family and friends, where appropriate. No final decision about disposal of residents' homes or property should be made until after the first review.

To offer an alternative type of residential care, consideration should be given to setting up a supported lodgings scheme in the division. This would probably necessitate the appointment of a social services officer, preferably full-time, to set up and run the scheme.

Roles of staff and volunteers Clear operational objectives should be set for each establishment and individual worker.

Residential staff should be given more responsibility for the deployment of staff within the home and the use of financial allocations.

Some logistic functions should be transferred elsewhere.

The roles of deputy officer in charge and third officer should be examined.

The role of the residential and day care officer Consideration should be given to the appropriateness of the present roles and structure. Two alternatives were suggested:

i. to retain the present basic structure and to clarify roles and functions;

ii. to develop an alternative structure whereby one social services manager, or other senior post, is made responsible for all the residential and day care officers.

Within these two alternatives there were several variables. There could be a geographical split different from the present areas, or there could be specialisation according to client groups. The latter alternative was carefully considered and rejected.

The residential and day care officer role or its equivalent should be brought nearer to divisional management and should have more influence on policy decisions. Much clarification of the role was required, particularly as it concerned the needs of the officers in charge for management and support.

Whatever structure was developed the workload of each residential and day care officer must be considered. Each should be responsible for about eight units, and responsibility for voluntary and private units would be an additional factor. Consideration should also be given to salary grades and status appropriate to the task, and to support, including clerical help in particular.

Wardens of sheltered housing Thought should be given to the appropriate role of the warden in sheltered accommodation, bearing in mind the purpose of the accommodation and the level of dependence of the tenants.

Volunteers In the interests of clients there should be more use of volunteers directly by social services and suitable tasks should be defined. It is unlikely that this will be achieved without the appointment of a volunteer organiser and the creation of such a post should be considered. This person would be responsible for recruiting and inducting volunteers, supporting social workers in using them and evaluating the work of the volunteers.

The use of volunteers to assist home helps should be explored.

Each home for the elderly should be encouraged to build up a bank of volunteers, and residential staff given support in developing this idea. It would also be advisable to attach volunteers to sheltered accommodation complexes. The housing department might make a contribution to the post of volunteer organiser.

The nature and method of payment of expenses to volunteers should be examined and if possible simplified.

Consideration should be given to the stimulation of schemes of self help in selected neighbourhoods as a means of helping the frail elderly living alone.

Training and staff support More training and support should be provided for residential staff.

More positive support should be offered to residential staff by residential and day care officers and senior social workers.

An intensive training scheme should be launched for all staff concerned with the elderly, but particularly for residential staff. This scheme should be based in the division and should include:
induction training for all staff.
continued training in skills and knowledge.
study of mourning.
special training for senior residential staff.
understanding of different values and objectives.

While information and training seminars were seen as useful ways of achieving this, other ways should also be explored, training exercises, eg joint seminars to look at role of volunteers and boundaries.

Staff should receive training in the task of assessment.

A divisional training officer for residential staff should be appointed.

Regular staff meetings should be held in residential homes, and there should be a review of the frequency and functions of staff meetings in some homes.

Putting the principles into practice – The problems of change [the second seminar, February 1978]

The views expressed below come from the second seminar held in February 1978, when some doubts were beginning to be expressed about the manner in which change was being brought about.

Some people felt uncomfortably exposed in their daily work by the amount of change they found going on around them. Others seethed with frustration at what they saw as the snail-like pace at which things were actually changing. Quite a lot of this comes through in the summary of the discussions which follow.

In contrast to the earlier seminar now, on the whole, members' attention turned to putting into practice principles thrashed out during the previous year. How was the new style of care to be implemented and what effect would it have on workers as well as on the elderly themselves? The comments which follow address these matters. Once again only a selection of the total discussions is represented here, and comments are grouped under headings.

The process of change In the second seminar the review of the year's work since the start of the development exercise predictably produced some divergence of opinion. One group agreed there had been positive moves forward; another expressed disappointment at the apparent lack of progress.

In some quarters there was a sense of frustration: a feeling that management staff were too often diverted from the declared goals by outside influences, whether financial, pressure from the media, the current emphasis on work with children, or a need to react to crises at the expense of general development and evolution. On the other hand one group had clearly experienced a sense of pressure at the speed of change and expressed anxiety about the extent to which change should be imposed. Some considered that gradual evolution might be more desirable.

The residents' responses to change was also noted. Some of them, after many years in residence, simply did not welcome change. The attitude of a proportion of residents and relatives could be summed up in the comment: 'After all, they are paid to look after us, aren't they?'

The bringing together of representatives from various working groups and then setting them to work at a common task had played an important part in the process of the project and, indeed, in the process of change. All groups felt the open atmosphere thus produced had been highly beneficial. It led to each group of workers gaining a better understanding of the others' problems and an improved level of communication. Health service members, though, regretted that their service had not been more adequately represented, and were particularly sorry that few representatives from the medical profession had been present. They had felt this lack most keenly in the working groups and considered the content of the reports reflected this imbalance. The care assistants, however, were gratified that, almost for the first time, their views had been sought and valued.

Risk-taking This important subject came up in the context of both field and residential work. It was agreed that risk taking in no sense implied taking foolish chances with the health and wellbeing of clients but was rather the exercise of judgement, based upon experience and training, of what was possible for the client to attempt in life. When there was any degree of doubt about the client's abilities, whether in such things as self-catering at home or boiling a kettle in a residential establishment, it was considered to be especially important to have help readily available from such people as neighbours, relatives and voluntary workers.

Assessment, allocation and reviews Sensitive assessment, it was maintained, has a number of attributes. It is not a once-and-for-all exercise but the starting point for a continuous review of the client's needs. Successful assessment matched the client's needs to the resources available and this, in its turn, should then become valuable data for management and the allocation of resources.

The pilot project on inter-professional assessment, using a revised assessment form, had proved to be an issue of intense interest – especially the dramatic reduction in recommendations for residential care once alternative methods of meeting need had been regularly discussed by the team. There were nevertheless some reservations about this, and some seminar members thought that in certain instances such alternatives might not prove successful. Ultimately residential care might prove to be the only practical solution to the problem, but, at least, it was no longer a foregone conclusion that an application would lead to a limited range of options being considered. The most exciting feature of this project had been that it had proved possible to identify and mobilise a great deal of community support which had previously lain untapped.

Inter-professional assessment had highlighted the poorly developed liaison arrangements between the social services and housing departments, especially in regard to the selection of tenants for sheltered housing and transfers of tenants from sheltered housing to residential care. Housing representatives feared that as tenants became more frail they would require as much care as residents in homes for the elderly.

It was therefore vital to establish jointly agreed criteria for the different types of accommodation.

A suggestion was made that staff from different agencies could, with advantage, exchange jobs or be attached to each other for a period. In this way a better understanding might be established about the tasks in each service.

The desirability of introducing regular reviews of all residents in homes for the elderly was debated with vigour. Some thought that even if staff time and other factors were to allow such a thing to happen undue fears might be aroused in a few residents' minds by such reviews.

Maybe the gradual introduction of reviews of new residents would be better – or perhaps regular exchanges between the community, residential care and sheltered accommodation would work. But such a course would presuppose that links between departments had been successfully forged; at present they were too slender to sustain these ideas. A similar pattern to that which obtains in child care might prove to be best. This would imply some form of continuous assessment, wherever the client might be living, and in this way resources would be fully used and new needs could be identified.

Fieldwork Dismay was expressed that, despite the thought and work undertaken since the first seminar, fieldwork for the elderly remained largely the province of social services officers and was still rarely taken on by qualified social workers. The social workers regretted this but pointed out that as long as the current emphasis on work with children was perpetuated, whatever their own inclinations, there was little likelihood that they would be in a position to include elderly clients in their caseloads. Discussion tended to emphasise that more resources would be the solution, but the desire of fieldworkers to spend time in working with elderly clients was also called in question. Blaming the lack of resources could be an escape route. A more imaginative approach might improve the situation without extra resources, and this should include more use of volunteers and voluntary organisations.

One group discussed the question of having a social worker with responsibility solely for boarding out elderly clients. If this could be arranged for children, why not for the elderly? The local health authority had specialist health visitors for elderly clients, whereas social services devolved this work to the non-specialist social services officers. Perhaps the residential home might become the base for specialist workers and in this way it would both develop their workers' skills and prevent homes becoming 'outposts' of the department. Without a doubt it could hardly fail to change attitudes towards social work with this client group.

There still remained a keenly felt gap between residential and field-workers (although instances were cited of the staff of homes becoming more involved in case reviews). Fieldworkers said they knew little about clients in residential establishments; in some instances they even felt excluded and had to fight for information.

Gradually the view emerged that, try as they might, this problem was not something that could easily be overcome by individual workers. Was it not time for some centrally-sponsored project, perhaps undertaken by a development officer or team, to initiate a new approach to this vexed and long-standing question. Perhaps the 'key worker' pattern could give a lead, or the introduction of monitored experiments with social workers based in residential homes. Certainly more needed to be done to identify and mobilise what was going on in the community: sometimes social workers did not look far beyond their own department and missed out on the initiatives such as those made by less formal groups. A more radical development project would be in a position to test out the way new patterns of field, residential and voluntary care functioned and in this way bring them into closer working harmony than had so far proved possible. This in itself should evolve new patterns of care for the elderly.

Day care Despite the definition put forward by the working party, and endorsed by some, a universally acceptable concept of day care remained elusive. In the course of the discussions the full gamut of the seminar members' experience was explored. Certainly there was a need for day centres but, to avoid a long drive for only a few hours at the centre more and smaller centres nearer to peoples' homes were needed. Day care should be a full day out and available throughout the week and there was as much, if not more, need for this facility to be open at the weekends, when loneliness was often acute because elderly people were easily overlooked by the rest of the community at this time. Sitting rooms in sheltered housing might be called into use to serve this purpose.

The link between day care and residential care was much discussed. There were obviously conflicts between the needs of residents, who should be able to feel the establishment is their home and that they have the normal rights of privacy, their own territory and peace, and the day care clients' needs for conversation and new relationships along with a change of scene and different activities.

It was not easy to define who might need day care. Many elderly people had relatives who did not undertake the roles which might obviate the need for such a service. Perhaps more could be done to harness volunteers and other community resources and help them to take day care principles into peoples' own homes. Day care usually implied clients going to a building provided by a statutory or voluntary organisation, with paid staff in attendance. It was all too easy to follow the traditional path and assume that the service had to be provided in this way. Maybe more could be achieved by a different approach.

Transport Transport, so vital for effective day care, proved an intractable subject. Basically it seemed there was a shortage of the right kinds of vehicles (with tailgate and lift for wheelchairs) and that the service, which included the cost of an attendant as well as a driver, was becoming too expensive.

Provided expenses, petrol costs and insurance were given due attention more voluntary transport could be mobilised for those able to travel in cars or minibuses. It was unfortunate in this respect that a single volunteer could not always cope alone with a disabled person who might have to negotiate steps or steep slopes, whilst a person living upstairs might need the skilled help of an ambulanceman to get him down to a waiting vehicle.

Better use might be made of departmental vehicles. They could be used during slack periods and the possibility of using other departments' vehicles and the expertise of the Brighton transport manager should be explored. New ideas and new sources of help should be sought.

Residential staff felt that the use of public transport was necessarily limited by the frailty of many of their residents. In addition the cost of bus travel kept many of the elderly housebound and out of touch with friends and relatives. New policies such as the greater emphasis on day and community care and the encouragement of activity amongst elderly people were bound to put increased burdens on the transport services which were often sadly insufficient. On the other hand some of the transport difficulties might be reduced as day centres became more local.

Residential care As so many of the seminar members were employed in homes for the elderly or had related management responsibilities it was inevitable that residential care should be the focus of much attention. One of the fundamental questions at issue was the nature of residential work with the elderly and the possibility for some residents of rehabilitation into the community. It seemed realistic to hope that some elderly residents might be able to resume life in the community after a period in residential care when their physical condition had improved and they had recovered sufficient confidence to practice the basic skills of living. Questions were asked about having a specialised rehabilitation unit, and whether long-term care should only be considered for those who were unable to respond to a programme of rehabilitation. It was also suggested that if rehabilitation were to play a key role residential homes could become the central point for assessment and for support to community services.

If rehabilitation were to become a primary goal of residential work this principle should also apply to those who, perforce, had to remain in residence. They too should derive some benefit from a programme of rehabilitation. In carrying this out careful assessment would be required. If residents were to perform at their optimum level such an assessment would need to demonstrate those tasks they found difficult as well as those they could still do, so that they could be helped to discover alternative methods of coping with problems.

There was also a great deal of debate about the central issue of risk-taking – this useful phrase which, at times, itself risked becoming a catch-phrase! It was thought that risk-taking must imply the most careful observation by the staff of each individual's capacities. Sensitivity and understanding would be required so that pressure was not put on residents to perform beyond their capacities. Risk-taking should never be allowed to deteriorate into foolhardiness which might lead to nervousness, accidents and regression.

The elderly mentally infirm were seen to pose a special problem and there was considerable difference of opinion as to the advisability of including a substantial number of such residents in homes for less disabled people. Their needs on the one hand were not in tune with the ideas being developed in this project. Against this it had been demonstrated elsewhere that greater interaction between residents could lead to more mutual care and less rapid deterioration. However, examples were known of one or two mentally disturbed residents who had disrupted a group of residents as a whole. There had to be a balance of lifestyles, and difficult decisions had to be made showing respect for the general tolerance level of all the residents in the home. It was anticipated that this problem would undoubtedly get worse. As community care improved those who came into care were likely to be more frail, and more mentally confused people would probably be included in their number.

Staffing was touched on and it was considered vital that staffing ratios should be maintained if alternative lifestyles in the homes were to prove possible. A different balance in the grades employed might prove necessary, and it would be essential that staff were of good calibre and carefully recruited, and that appropriate amounts of support and training were provided.

It became quite plain that seminar members were now, almost automatically, perceiving residential care as part of the whole rather than an end in itself. If fieldwork services, domiciliary services, health care, day care, sheltered housing and transport, along with residential care, were seen as articulating parts of the whole, homes for the elderly would no longer be encapsulated in their own private world. In these circumstances the pace of development was bound to be variable and in a constant state of flux. Successful changes inside the homes must inevitably depend a good deal on changes outside.

Attention was turned to changes taking place in the day-to-day living of the residents. Questions of choice and control were central to this issue. The matter of making residents responsible for their own drugs symbolised this problem and was often central to the discussion. It seemed an 'all or nothing' policy could readily take over here, but as with most other problems discussed, individualising the staff's response to the residents' abilities to deal with their drugs was the key.

Recent changes in residential care Having spent a year in discussion, experiment and working groups everyone was full of ideas, and there was a strong desire to move forward to new lifestyles and new policies.

A list was made of changes which had already come about in residential care and it proved to be quite impressive:

the introduction of facilities for making tea and snacks;
changes in mealtimes;
flexible hours for meals;
choice of menus;
smaller group tables;
changed methods of service;
the introduction of craft sessions;
residents' choice of outings and activities;

the consultation of residents on decoration and furnishings;
the proposed introduction of lockable personal cupboards;
the introduction of small group living.

Training Good staff selection must, everyone considered, necessarily be followed by appropriate training. As new staff quickly took their line from existing patterns it was imperative that attitudes and responses should be discussed and explored at an early stage. Induction programmes should therefore be organised. There was some debate as to whether these should be carried out inside the homes or elsewhere. Some care assistants felt there could be advantage in bringing staff together from various homes. If officers in charge were to be the ones to organise these programmes they themselves were likely to require help in learning how to teach and in perceiving each individual worker's pattern of learning.

Training for care assistants was, at present, thought to be inadequate and insufficient. They were pitched in at the deep end and left to get on with it. They pointed out that, whatever might be official policy, they were expected to carry out quasi-nursing techniques for which they were not equipped and which went beyond their job description. To pretend this did not happen made both staff and residents very vulnerable. The should, they felt, receive systematic instruction in the basic practical skills such as lifting and bathing. Since reorganisation there were growing health service resources which could be used for training in these skills.

In-service study was seen to be as important as induction training. It could, perhaps, be most effective when, rather than sending one or two workers at a time to a distant centre, the entire staff group in a home were involved in the training periods. Seminars could then be tailormade to one particular establishment, and everyone from the head to the handyman included. Staff meetings in which practices and attitudes to work were also discussed would be an important complement to such sessions.

The lack of common training for field and residential workers was deplored. If this was substantially increased much progress could be made. Concepts such as that of 'key worker', which assumes that roles are interchangeable, would be better discussed in this context. A common professional base would enable residential workers to carry caseloads and to take on the 'key worker' role alongside fieldwork colleagues. In these discussions it soon became clear that most participants deplored the inequalities in training opportunities for field and residential workers. Indeed, it was apparent that staff of homes for the elderly were not adequately trained to undertake the range of work expected of them. If their roles were to develop, as envisaged by the project, a systematic training programme must be arranged.

In all the groups the situation was always changing and lively, each day producing new developments, new problems, new achievements.

Changes in lifestyle

Changes in long standing patterns of care do not come about without a great deal of thinking and hard work and this was the case in Brighton.

It often happens that the final push towards experiment and change comes through individual initiative. In this case the officers in charge of two homes for the elderly in Brighton, Hazel Court and Beechwood House, decided to introduce group living in their establishments. The paths they took in implementing these decisions were quite different and the reports of their experience make interesting reading.

Although personal initiative played its part when the two homes changed to group living, the experiment would not have got far without support from others. In addition to the support available from the residential and day care officers the Development Group arranged for a former principal officer for residential services from another county to advise and support these homes during the changes for a period of six months ending in July 1978.

The reports which follow are compiled from notes made by members of staff in each home and by the adviser.

One of the residential and day care officers kept a diary of events and this comes next. It is a mixture of details about fittings and fixtures and the people involved in the home, laced with the frustration of co-ordinating events when no-one turns up to fix things at the appointed time.

The last part of this chapter deals with another experiment, that of the 'key worker' which was introduced at another home for the elderly in Brighton, Chestnut Lodge. Because of the number of different workers who may attend to their needs, an elderly person in residential care can all too readily have the sensation that there is no one person primarily concerned about him. The experiment at Chestnut Lodge consisted in giving the responsibility for all aspects of the care of each individual to one care assistant. This personalised or 'key worker' virtually became 'their' residents' guardian.

Small group living in Hazel Court

Hazel Court is a purpose-built home with thirty-two beds built in 1953. It is situated on an estate near shops and a pub, and there is a good bus service into Brighton. The home has two storeys and is built on traditional lines, with wide corridors, several sitting rooms and sitting areas, a large dining room and a kitchen which, prior to the appointment of the present officer in charge, was out of bounds to all but the kitchen staff.

The officer in charge wished to move away from the traditional method of caring for residents in large groups, and decided she would introduce small group living when facilities became available. The staff were anxious about the coming changes, but the enthusiasm of the officer in charge communicated itself to them as she explained her hopes and discussed possible problems with them.

Meetings of staff and residents took place prior to the changes to keep everyone in the picture, and relatives and friends of residents were also informed.

The first group officially started in January 1978. It comprised six residents, four of whom had shown an immediate interest in the group living scheme when the idea was first introduced to staff and residents in the preceding year. These four got on well together and were already much involved in the day-to-day household activities and chores. They looked forward to the change as a means of gaining privacy more than anything else. It was suggested that they should choose the remaining two residents for the group, and this they did.

During the first week there were few problems and little staff help was needed. Most of the group had become familiar with the electric kettle in the preceding months elsewhere in the house. They soon became familiar with the toaster and hostess trolley and they replenished their supplies each morning by visiting the main kitchen.

Towards the middle of the second week, after the initial excitement and the early achievements, it became clear that some of the group were missing the general hubbub of the rest of the house. The group's sitting room was on the first floor at the end of the corridor and, although it was a bright room with French windows leading onto a large balcony, it was somewhat cut off from the main lounge and dining room on the ground floor. Instead of using their own group room some of them were choosing to sit in the main entrance hallway, which had armchairs and a settee.

The staff now assumed a supportive and encouraging role by making themselves available to sit down and talk with and listen to the group, reassuring them that they had not been rejected. At this time also the Christmas party was arranged, and friends, relatives and neighbours were invited to it in addition to residents and staff. This event helped them to realise that they were not isolated.

From the outset it was evident that there was a clash of personalities between the two dominant women in the group. As their arguments became more frequent it caused some distress to the rest of the group and, although both had been good friends prior to this, it was difficult to see how to bring about a happy compromise. It was then decided that this was an opportune time to commence the next group, and one of the women in the first group was asked to help form it, using her experiences of the previous month. She agreed to do this.

The second group started in February 1978. It consisted of the woman from the first group, a man and a married couple who had been admitted the previous week and shown little desire to mix with any of the other residents. They had brought with them their bed, their colour TV and armchairs for their bedroom so they had a virtually self-contained bedsitter. The wife had been in hospital for a year and the husband welcomed the opportunity of doing all he could for her.

The second group room was small and at first glance not ideally suited. Most facilities were provided, including a radio, but there was no room for a TV set. The chosen group were eager and willing to give it a try, on the understanding that television viewing would be shared with the first group which was next door. Temporarily their washing up was done in the laundry room opposite, but it was hoped this could soon be converted into a fitted kitchen.

The 'leading lady' in this group caused a problem because she talked so much. The married couple found this difficult to cope with, but after discussing it together eventually they all decided to give it another try.

The first group was proceeding well when after two months the dominant woman suddenly became ill and died. The effect on the others was overwhelming. As well as suffering the grief of losing a close friend, they floundered because of the loss of her practical attributes. She had been the one they depended on to organise things; and now there seemed no one capable of taking the responsibility and it seemed wrong to introduce a new member immediately. The staff made a concerted effort to support them over this difficult period and to help them to find their feet. Gradually another woman emerged as the leader and they were soon able to resume their happy routine.

In April an atmosphere of frustration and unrest among staff and residents was caused because the introduction of further groups was hampered by delays in structural alterations. There were occasional murmurings of discontent from members of the groups who viewed other residents in their hotel-like setting and perhaps longed to rejoin them. On the other hand, many of those not in groups envied the select facilities and privacy the groups enjoyed, and other residents felt great apprehension at the thought of change.

It was hoped that the next group of eight would move into their room when a sink unit had been installed, but the staff decided it would be wrong to wait any longer for the work to be done, and so a compromise was reached. The new group occupied what was formerly a four-bedded room on the ground floor. It converted very well to a sitting room at one end and a dining area at the other end, with two tables each seating four. Temporarily the washing up was done in part of the main kitchen, which was already partitioned off.

These eight people proved to be in need of a great deal of supervision as only two were physically and mentally capable. The others, as well as needing some form of walking aid, lacked concentration, and it was found necessary at first to allocate one member of staff permanently to this group. The first week was rather chaotic, and although a work rota was instigated, two of the women constantly squabbled and complained that they were doing all the work. It was interesting to note how these people had sat together in the conventional set-up before moving to group living and had, on the surface, got on well together without saying much. When they were thrown together in a situation where communication became necessary, in the early stages this contact was of a quarrelsome nature.

After about a month, slowly some semblance of order emerged. This came about for two reasons. Firstly one man took charge of the heated trolley and the tea-making, which suited the rest as they were rather timid with the appliances. Secondly, one of the dominant women took responsibility for the daily ordering of provisions. This group, for some reason, took a long time to settle down, with frequent disputes and flare-ups. Impromptu meetings often had to be held, chaired by one of the residential staff, to ease the tensions, and the group was in need of fairly constant staff support.

In all the groups the situation was always changing and lively, each day producing new developments, new problems, new achievements.

As well as residents growing and gaining confidence from the staff, the staff found that they were learning from the residents. On several occasions, decisions reached by staff discussions were totally rejected by residents in favour of their own solutions. For example, a work rota which the officer in charge had considered helpful was criticised by one group, and the more forceful and active members decided to take it upon themselves to deal with the workload personally. In another group one timid woman developed dramatically as a leader when a Belling cooker was produced for the group's use, and her culinary flair in producing exotic dishes was displayed several times a week.

It was interesting that few residents took the option of 'lying-in' in the mornings and only one made a habit of it. Elderly people seemed to prefer a set routine and breakfast at 8.30 am seemed to start the day right for them. After some discussion, it was also decided that they preferred the night staff to make a cup of tea at 7.00 am and a drink in the late evening, so these services were retained for those who wished to take advantage of them. Meal times were considerably altered, making them later in the day, and therefore maintaining more evening activities. This meant a considerable change in staff duties, with, for example, night staff not starting to rouse residents in the early hours, but concentrating only on those who required assistance in dressing and leaving other chores to the day staff. Correspondingly evening staff took on duties which were previously undertaken by the night staff. Kitchen staff were accepting later duties to enable them to prepare a much later evening meal.

The groups ordered and collected provisions such as tea, coffee, bread, cereals, preserves, and cleaning materials. Many assisted in cleaning their own rooms, particularly those with single rooms, and all were encouraged to furnish their rooms, and to help plan colour schemes for group areas.

One gratifying aspect of the changes was the co-operation of the staff, who gradually became totally committed to group living and all it entailed (though at the outset some were sceptical and one care assistant thought it was cruel). Attitudes changed for the better all round and the officer in charge came to depend and rely on all levels of staff. The cook had to make great changes in her work routine and her volume of work actually increased.

It was also satisfying to see how residents used their initiative to develop new skills and to revive old ones, and how much pleasure they felt in their achievements. The residents began to see themselves again as individuals with minds of their own, and not as part of a mass of thirty-five people who had to be 'cared for'.

Small group living in Beechwood House

Beechwood House is a single storey home built in 1966 for thirty-five residents. It was extended in 1971 to take fifteen more residents with a two storey addition. Due to the terrain the lower level of this extension is downstairs and there is no lift, so limited use is made of this accommodation.

The home is in the middle of a surburban estate which is very hilly and difficult for elderly people. There appears to be little, if any, community spirit or activities. The home is designed around a series of nearly identical corridors with two inner courtyards. These corridors are very confusing and it is easy to get lost. The home was originally run on conventional lines, and the pattern of the day was firmly established, with the emphasis on 'quality of care' rather than 'quality of life'.

The officer in charge was eager to move into group living and well motivated to achieve this. She had two progressive young assistants who were both anxious to seek new ways of providing a better life for the residents, but the rest of the staff were apprehensive at the thought of change.

It became clear that a series of staff meetings, to discuss the concept of group living would be necessary to convince staff that it was worth trying. It was also clear there must be complete co-operation and agreement from all members of staff before the project could start, because they must fully understand their new role, how to achieve it, and what the effects might be for the residents.

There was a good deal of planning and preparatory work, to consider how the groups might be formed and where in the home they would be situated. The home was designed with many small sitting areas and these would form the basis of the lounges and dining rooms for the groups. It was also possible to create kitchen areas in odd corners, adapting sluices and cleaning cupboards and using to the full every available space. Extra socket outlets were needed for electric kettles, toasters and small cookers, and additional cupboard space was required to store provisions. Clearance had to be obtained from the Fire Prevention Officer (for kitchen areas) and the Environmental Health Officer (when sluices were converted).

To encourage the residents to be as independent as possible, kettles, toasters, refrigerators, storage facilities, small cookers, crockery, cutlery and linen were provided for each group.

This planning and preparation took place at Beechwood House before the residents were consulted about the changes, because the officer in charge wished to introduce group living for them all at the same time (the 'starting pistol' method) rather than in phases.

In the next stage discussions took place with residents about the concept of group living and their relatives were also involved in the discussions. The residents were apprehensive about changes of any kind and the thought of moving from their protected environment into a more independent role caused many problems. One resident asked, 'How can you expect me to do my own laundry?' and another stated quite definitely that she would not clean her own bedroom because she shared it with someone else. These comments seemed to reflect their fear of the unknown and how it would work. Staff prepared for the problems to come by spending time with residents and because of these close personal relationships residents became more confident they might be able to live more independently. All the residents were seen individually by the staff and considerable time was spent discussing the changes with them until gradually attitudes began to alter and some enthusiasm and curiosity was aroused.

Residents were told they would be able to choose when to get up, what to have for breakfast and when. They would serve their own lunch from a heated trolley which would be loaded in the kitchen; they could please themselves whether they wanted the meal or preferred to make their own arrangements, and they could generally act and think as independently as possible. They slowly began to accept that they would move from a large group of fifty into small groups of eight and that the groups would form the basis for their future lifestyle.

It was felt that relatives should be involved before the move into group living took place. They were therefore invited to a cheese and wine party and the idea of group living was explained to them. This was a highly successful event as it enabled relatives to express their fears, to discuss possible problems with staff, and to leave knowing that their elderly relatives would continue to receive staff support albeit in a different way.

All preparations having been made, the groups were chosen after a lot of careful thought, and they moved into their new areas. The task of the staff was now to support the groups and to encourage their independence. It was found that, despite losing many of their former traditional tasks, staff soon became fully involved with residents in more informal ways. They had time to sit and talk to them without feeling guilty and could meet their individual needs. A caring attitude quickly began to develop amongst the groups. The more able either took on extra tasks to support the less capable members or assisted them in these tasks.

The groups soon began to work well and to interact happily together. Few residents were unhappy with the situation and these were mainly those who had rejected communal living under the previous regime. They felt they were being asked to undertake tasks they considered should be done by staff. The majority of residents preferred the 'new way' to the old, and felt they were now part of the home and fully involved in its activities. The home became alive and active, groups chatted to each other and to the staff, who found this extremely rewarding.

During the first week breakfast time was very disorganised and caused everyone concern. This arose because residents were getting up at various times – there was no set routine and they were unsure of their own capabilities and what was expected of them. They wondered, for instance, whether they were responsible for the group or only for themselves. Residents had to be reassured that if other members of the group decided to lie in they must be responsible for getting their own breakfasts.

Lunchtime from the outset caused the least problems. Residents coped very well with the heated trolleys, apart from a 'trolley jam' on the first day when the residents came with their pre-heated trolleys to collect the food. The routine was subsequently changed and trolleys were heated and fully prepared in the kitchen ready for collection at 12.30 pm. An amusing incident occurred one lunchtime when one group served the apple crumble as a second vegetable!

During the first week five of the seven groups needed very little supervision. Each group developed at a different pace, with leaders and followers, grumblers and helpers emerging in most of them. Many residents showed unexpected qualities, and many conflicts and upsets had to be dealt with sympathetically by the staff.

Very few changes amongst group members needed to take place, and groups proved surprisingly understanding in coping with the less capable,frail and senile members. Gradually group members adopted roles and undertook regular tasks as routine became established.

Initially the problems of staff were similar to those of the residents. The changeover meant a change of timetable and routine and it was confusing at first. In addition the staff had to confront the residents more, to meet them as people and generally to have more contact with them. This contact meant using skills to deal with individual personalities and individual reactions to the same problem. Staff members were doubtful at times if any progress was being made and found it difficult to be objective about the situation.

At the end of the third week a staff meeting was held to discuss problems and observations. It was agreed that in spite of some doubts the groups had made progress and some changes in attitude were noticed. Far more initiative was being used by the residents and they were becoming less reliant on staff to organise and distribute tasks within the groups. Only one group still needed tactfully organising. One of the group members had complained that a lot of arguing went on which made her nervous. However the staff realised that this group needed a lot of support, because of the diversity of personalities within it, and it was recognised that problems might be inherent with this group and that they would need more supervision than the others.

Staff noted that some residents initially thought the changeover was a temporary measure, a familiar question being, 'How long is this going to last?' These residents seemed to think that if the group living was not a success the home would revert to the old system.

Some members of staff felt that morning and afternoon drinks should be provided by the staff for the less able residents. For a variety of reasons not all the residents were in their sitting rooms when groups made their coffee and tea arrangements, and this meant that some handicapped residents were not getting a drink. There was some concern that if the staff did this it might be difficult to justify it to the other residents, and this could cause unnecessary problems at this early stage. It was decided to observe the situation closely during the following weeks and discuss it again later. During this discussion members of staff raised the question of a 'total care group'. This would be a group made up of the less able residents who could receive consistent total care from the staff, and thereby relieve the other residents of this responsibility. The staff were divided on this point. It was felt by some that by integrating the groups the residents were becoming more aware and concerned for each other, and that to isolate the less able ones defeated one of the aims of group living, which was respect and concern for the individual. Some thought it was unfair that so many residents should have this responsibility, and considered that staff should care for these residents more fully as a separate group. It was decided that integrated groups should be given a fair trial and an alternative discussed, if necessary, at a later date.

Mealtimes were more sociable than previously. It was a pleasure to hear the residents conversing and to see them involved in the general hubbub at mealtimes.

The risks involved with group living were uppermost in the minds of the staff, particularly the risk of fire. They had some reassurance on this point, however, as the fire alarm went off at the same time on two consecutive days. It was discovered that the culprit was not, as suspected, a faulty alarm system, but burnt toast picked up by the sensitiser in the hall adjoining the kitchen. Residents were later advised to clear the crumbs regularly from their toasters!

Another development which gave staff some encouragement was the care one group showed for one of their members who was ill and confined to his room. His meals and drinks were prepared for him and the staff were asked to take them along to his room.

After the first few weeks it could be said that groups were more organised and more confident and progress in a practical sense was being made. Generally there seemed to be more awareness of each other's needs and in some cases genuine compassion. There was more verbal communication generally and even when this took the form of grumbling to anyone prepared to listen such as staff, visitors and social workers, it was felt that this was a positive reaction and preferable to no reaction at all. There was also less concern and fewer complaints about physical ailments.

Diary of the residential and day care officer

9 December 1977 Spoke to officer-in-charge after the visit of the Development Group's consultant to discuss the following points:

1. To consider seven groups of seven rather than eight groups of six residents.
2. Use of sluice as washing-up area.
3. Should trolleys be stored in the kitchen or living areas?
4. Kitchenettes suggested rather than washing-up areas.

12 December Visited Beechwood House to re-assess washing-up areas. Officer in charge considering use of room dividers and liaising with supplies division re heated trolleys.

Contact made with environmental health officer.

19 December Visited with environmental health officer: sluice must be sealed off. Arranged joint visit with architect.

23 December Environmental health officer and architect agree on washing-up arrangement; there must be a slope on draining board covering sluice.

12 January 1978 Verbal estimate for twin outlets on TV aerial points.

16 January Authority has been given for expenditure at Beechwood House.

28 January Orders placed for necessary works. Purchased room dividers.

17 February Changed the order for food trolleys; now ordering standard trolleys with heated cupboards which fit on top.

28 February 1½ hour staff meeting on group living during which I was able to feed back from a county meeting with representatives from another county which has changed to small group living.

Tender sent out for electrical work.

1 March Officer in charge held further staff meeting today and is concerned about involving evening and night shift staff.

6 March There was a report on Radio Brighton and in the local paper on possible developments at Beechwood House. Discovered that a press statement was issued following a routine report on the exercise to the Social Services Committee. Regret that the local effect was not foreseen and we were not consulted.

Visited and discussed with officer in charge. She and staff will inform residents tomorrow.

Expedite purchase of toasters, kettles and other equipment.

7 March Visited. Residents in general quite enthusiastic and staff are quite encouraged. One resident told one of the staff that she would not be needed soon as the residents would be looking after themselves.

10 March Architect's department will now put work in hand but has the Fire Officer approved change of use and 'cooking' in other areas? Discussed principles of group living with the Fire Officer who will visit next week.

28 March Officer in charge reports satisfactory progress. There is some apprehension, although most residents are accepting the proposals.

Date for change fixed for 4 April

No sign of electricians, architects will chase.

Only one care assistant is not prepared to alter her hours to 7.30 am instead of 8.00 am at weekends.

Who pays for TVs – amenities or division? Raise with management team. Fire Officer has approved arrangements.

29 March Fire Officer telephoned. He is recommending fire doors to be half fire resisting doors and the South Side washing-up area may have to have a smoke stop.

Electrical contractor cannot start work until 10 April so the change over date must be put back.

30 March Wine and cheese party this evening. Sixteen relatives, twelve staff, three officers. The Development Group's consultant and several managers attended. Very successful occasion and much goodwill ensued. It was encouraging for staff and they were able to talk freely.

31 March Expressed my concern to architect about the delay in electrical work but as this was over £300 it had to go out to tender. The delay is frustrating as I have been harassing him since January. Reported progress to divisional director.

6 April Attended forum for professional staff at County Hall on group living with officer in charge of Beechwood House.

10 April Very useful visit to home in Eastbourne Division run on group living lines with officer in charge and six staff from Beechwood House. Very good for staff morale, who now find group living not nearly so daunting as they imagined.

Electrical contractor started work!

13 April Agreed to provision of two more TV sets.

Changeover date changed to Tuesday 18 April

Sufficient staff and friends are available to help with physical re-organisation.

The Development Group's consultant has visited again and is pleased with progress.

17 April Spoke to many residents and staff about tomorrow's change, no adverse attitudes at all.

Everyone of staff is keyed up and ready to go!

Re fire precautions letter which arrived today, staff are concerned that self-closing doors of washing areas will be too restricting for the residents. They are seeking assurance that if doors are hooked back staff will not be reprimanded.

18 April Group living commenced.

3.00 pm visited. Five groups started very well. One doubtful and has problems. One chaotic! The last group of five was reduced to one as four went to their bedrooms. I chatted to one man left. His attitude was 'I am not paying £37.50 per week and have to cook my own breakfast, push this trolley etc.'.. By this time we have found some milk for him (he was trying to get himself an afternoon cup of tea) he was a bit more amiable. Later he was directing one of 'his' ladies to the tea room. She was being a bit awkward too about finding the tea room. We kept out of it and they sorted themselves out. To add to minor problems the vicar phoned and said he would arrive in twenty-five minutes for his service. This meant re-organising the dining room group and asking their agreement to the service being held there. This may have to be the pattern for small group activities like church services. Problem arose of transferring tea pots, milk, hot water etc. from preparation rooms to living area.

One staff volunteered a gift of a food trolley and arrangements made to borrow one from another home. A manager visited, together with the county development officer and residential co-ordinator.

19 April Delivered trolley early (8.45 am). Officer in charge a little disorganised; almost everyone had breakfast and she still had their pills.

21 April Visited Beechwood House at 9.15 am for informal staff meeting on daily progress. As all staff are watching reactions of all groups, different ideas come out. One resident was seen to be a very disruptive influence in a particular group and it was felt she should be moved. Discussion took place on whether this should happen.

It was interesting that the groups themselves were encouraging and supporting care of their members to do something and even saying, 'You can do better than that'. The staff role here was to ensure the resident was not pushed too far.

Discussion also on certain residents monopolising jobs and thus causing possible weakness to the group in that the person becomes indispensable – if sick or suddenly unwilling the group will have a problem. Staff will monitor groups and self imposed as distinct from'group agreed' tasks.

The staff are going to start recording residents' attitudes and things that they see or hear, and compare notes. Follow-up will continue as in the past (recorded in duty book).

These meetings will continue every few days for a time.

Geriatrician has been invited to visit.

Extra TV sets not arriving until Monday next. The delay in ordering was because endeavours were being made to get gift sets. (In future planning possible gifts should be assembled or canvassed very early on in the planning, such things as TVs, odd tables, food trolleys, even toasters and kettles might well be forthcoming). However two people offered to loan sets for the weekend. The residents in the groups were not in the least concerned and were quite happy to wait until next week. Maybe we attach too much importance to such accepted creature comforts.

24 April Officer in charge reports a fairly good though exhausting weekend. Three of the groups are going very well, two fairly well, and two need a lot of support and encouragement.

26 April One resident moved from a group that was too big for the available space.

3 May Visited with architect to discuss fire precautions. Suggest magnetic catches for some doors. Staff report that fire alarm has gone off on three mornings running at about 8.30 am – each time due to smoke from one toaster (resident likes burnt toast) that has been sited too close to a detector – replace by heat detector?

5 May Attended a staff meeting at Beechwood House with residential co-ordinator. Discussed a paper prepared by a care assistant about progress in various groups and the attitudes of both residents and staff. The questions of domestic hours was discussed. The reason for changing them was in anticipation of a later breakfast and the need of some involvement at midday mealtime. As events have gone the domestic assistants find that their varied half hour would be better used earlier in the day (ie 8.00 am) than between 1.00–1.30 pm.

The cook too finds that working until 6.00 pm is unnecessary and earlier arrival might be advantageous.

The staff thought that the half-dozen residents who might form an intensive care group should be absorbed by the seven groups.

The original grouping has worked well but in an effort to meet the difficulties envisaged with one man one group was overloaded, with three residents unable to contribute much.

The question of privacy for the group in the former dining room is causing some concern.

Thoughts so far:
1. The level of co-operation from other departments or sections must be fairly high in the initial stages. The connections at residential and day care officer level are not powerful enough to overcome set-backs (eg the electrical work was negotiated at the wrong level).
2. Logistically one can order the large things; many small things which make for added comfort can easily be missed (eg identification of each group's belongings – odd spare tables or chairs, extra small trolleys to collect forgotten things like sugar, cups etc).

Chestnut Lodge – an experiment with a 'key worker'

Chestnut Lodge is the largest home for the elderly in East Sussex. It was adapted from four large Victorian houses built about one hundred years ago. The home is situated in the centre of Brighton but, although it is only five minutes' walk from the town's major shopping centre, the advantage of this is considerably reduced because the home is built on a steep hill. There is accommodation for eighty-two elderly ladies. Many of the first residents came from the former workhouse establishments in the town.

Few residents are able to have a room to themselves as the following table shows:

Number of beds in each room	Number of rooms
1	8
2	9
3	10
4	5
6	1

The two small units within the home, with fifteen beds and ten beds respectively, are both arranged for group living, whereas the larger section still operates on traditional lines, with each sitting room accommodating fifteen to twenty residents, all sitting elbow to elbow. Fifty-seven people live in this section, and only four are engaged in any form of independent living. These four ladies share what used to be a staff flat and enjoy the privacy and independence that this allows.

Staff ratio The total establishment for care assistants is 820 hours plus 80 hours for night supervisors. This is broken down as follows:

Day staff		Night staff	
	11 @ 40 hrs		6 @ 40 hrs
	2 @ 35 hrs		2 night supervisors @ 40 hrs
	1 @ 30 hrs		
	2 @ 20 hrs		

Night supervisors hold the status of third officer and are responsible for their own team of three care assistants.

Organisation of the key worker scheme The key worker was a care assistant who took the major responsibility for the care of a group of residents. In deciding how to allocate residents to the key worker, it was agreed that established relationships between staff and residents must be respected and this was the basis for the formation of the groups. After further consultation with the staff the groups were completed by an equal distribution of independent, confused and 'difficult' residents. The groups varied between five and seven residents according to the hours worked by the care assistants.

The ideas behind the scheme were fully discussed with the staff to ensure that they understood their new tasks and that they were committed to the change. Notebooks were issued to each worker so that observations, along with relevant information discussed during supervision sessions or at the residents' annual reviews, could be recorded.

In order to allow the scheme to get started the care assistants' work had to be organised as effectively as possible. Demarcation lines had to be broken down and replaced by a more flexible routine, especially between day and night staff. Complete changes of routine were, for instance, required at night when residents were being assisted to bed and in the morning when they were getting up. It had been the day staffs' responsibility to help dependent residents to bed, with the result that all were in bed well before 8 pm. Consequently other residents felt obliged to go to bed at this hour too, because they did not wish to cause a disturbance by going later. Getting the residents up in the morning was done by the night staff and commenced with early morning tea between 5.30 am and 6.00 am, followed by a brisk routine of washing, dressing and coercing residents to be up and dressed by 8.00 am.

These rigid routines were not only bad for the residents, but, coming as they did at the end of a long shift, it was highly unlikely that staff would always exhibit patience and understanding when trying to complete their heavy duties. In addition it denied both staff and residents the opportunity of socialising during the evening.

The residents were consulted about the possibility of altering these routines and, although some scepticism was expressed, there was no resistance to the idea. Routines were therefore reversed and residents were helped into bed by the night staff from 9.00 pm onwards, and at the residents' request. Day staff assisted the residents to get up in the morning between 8.00 and 9.00 am. Interestingly, these changes were hardly noticed by the residents, but initially caused some problems for the staff.

Bedchanging arrangements were also altered. This was originally carried out over a period of four days but, with careful organisation plus the help of all available staff, it was later completed in one day. This gave workers more time to enjoy social activities with their residents and enabled them to have more control over the organisation of their work.

The function of the key worker An essential function of the key worker's role was her participation in the reviews of residents' progress. These commonly took place after their initial three months in residence, and were afterwards undertaken annually. It was found that these reviews not only greatly assisted the assessment of the elderly persons's progress and special needs but that they also enabled workers to evaluate their own performance. It was a new experience for care assistants to find that their opinions and observations were regularly required in a systematic way, and this developed their confidence and enhanced their commitment to working with the group.

The second basic principle of the scheme was to encourage the key worker to identify each member of her group as an individual with diverse abilities. In this way she empathised with her residents and learnt to recognise their needs and understand their pattern of behaviour. The care assistant concerned took over, where possible, all aspects of her residents' care and assumed responsibility for such things as choosing birthday and Christmas gifts, arranging shopping trips to buy clothes and organising transport for outings. In addition she arranged hospital, chiropody and hair appointments and made these at a time when it would be convenient for her to accompany the resident.

By working within this system the bond between the care assistant and the residents was inevitably strengthened. The care assistant derived greater satisfaction from her job and felt more involved in 'her' residents' total care. The obverse of this was that residents, too, developed a deeper interest in their care assistant and her family. Not only were the resident's horizons broadened but sharing experiences with the worker led to the development of a reciprocal rather than a dependent relationship between them.

The care assistants' detailed knowledge of their residents enabled them to utilise and develop every skill and interest the resident displayed, thus enhancing their abilities and, at times, appearing to arrest mental and physical deterioration. The more demanding residents will always pose a problem, because they necessitated a degree of extra attention whereas the less articulate person could easily be overlooked. However, under this scheme, the isolation of the less articulate was considerably reduced.

Visiting relatives showed approval of the scheme and many of them began to approach their care assistant directly about the resident's progress, and were eager to discuss problems with someone they knew had an individualised knowledge of their relative as well as a particular concern for her.

Staff found that his method of working added a new dimension to their daily routine. It also led them to become involved with residents when they were not on duty. Some visited residents in hospital during their time off, or took the trouble to provide the ingredients and cook someone's favourite recipe. Four members of staff supported a discharged resident in her own home by shopping and walking her dog.

Staff supervision Staff supervision played an important part in the functioning of the key worker scheme and should be built into the system on a regular basis. Supervision was offered to staff both individually and collectively. From the individual sessions it was possible to identify specific areas which might be causing concern, or perhaps highlight any misinterpretations of the home's policy. These could then be used in group training sessions designed for staff development.

A supervisory session sometimes began with a general discussion of each resident in the worker's group. Where there were problems possible causes of deterioration could be examined, alternative ways of meeting residents' needs considered and if necessary future programmes of care could be planned. Staff could also be helped to evaluate their role in relation to the success or failure of a treatment plan. Discussion might start with purely physical observations, such as cleanliness and continence and develop to cover all aspects of personal relationships, possible depression and the development of special interests.

This depth of care made very heavy demands upon staff and adequate support and supervision was essential. However, since the key worker scheme was introduced staff turnover and periods of sick leave were much reduced, and staff had more incentive in their work.

The main concern of our homes will be the quality of life of their residents.

Where are we now?

At the end of a project such as this the question 'Where are we now?' must inevitably arise. In order to achieve some understanding of this it can, in the first instance, be useful to look at where we have come from.

Over the last few decades the residential care of the elderly, in common with other groups, has moved from outmoded workhouse accommodation into more modern surroundings. Many of the staff caring for them have preferred to take responsibility for most aspects of the residents' lives, protecting them from dangers and regulating their day to day activities. They have not been alone in this view of the way in which care should be organised. As the interviews in the first chapter demonstrate, many potential residents anticipate that rules and regulations will be the order of the day in homes for the elderly.

These days it is becoming increasingly difficult for those charged with the responsibility for providing the caring services to keep pace with the rapidly changing values in society at large. Care of the elderly, like everything else, will always reflect these values, and the pace of change here will reflect the changes that nowadays take place daily in all our lives.

In some sense the workers engaged in this exercise were leading double lives. Whilst hard pressed in their day to day work to keep things going they were, at the same time, engaged in stretching and exercising themselves towards change. This was a difficult balancing act and one which involved considerable stress and strain.

At the final seminar the residential workers seemed a little breathless with the pace, although at times impatient at the length of time it had taken to get things altered. Other arms of the service conveyed the feeling that they were assembling at the starting line, waiting for the encouragement (and possibly resources) to enable them to take off in a new direction. Their gains so far had been in reorganising their administrative structure and, for the field workers, in seeing more clearly the role they might usefully play and what questions they should ask when, for instance, assessing an elderly person.

The project pointed afresh to the ways in which all aspects of care for the elderly were interlocked. It became evident that any changes in methods of residential work depended on alterations in the styles of care in the community and in day care, and, on a more local level, that more work needed to be done in bringing about closer relationships between the health and social services for elderly people in Brighton.

One of the main effects of this exercise was to examine the principles and practice of the care of the elderly. A big shift in thinking was symbolised by the distribution of the document entitled 'Residents' Rights' to each resident and staff member in the homes for the elderly in Brighton. This document was compiled by the managerial staff of the social services department after they had reflected on some of the written material arising from the Development Group project. It had some historical importance because it stated, contrary to the current expectations of many elderly people, that their basic rights as citizens would not be abrogated on entering residential care.

Obviously the ability of residents to take advantage of these rights varied greatly. Many, because of physical or mental frailty, would remain very dependent on the staff for their needs. The Residents' Rights document, however, helped create an environment in which all could have the opportunity to develop to their full potential. Quality of life was not accepted by all as being the most important element in residential care.

In the first part of this chapter there is a brief summary, under various headings, of some of the points which arose during the final seminar held at Brighton in March 1979. These comments are drawn from a number of speakers at that gathering but, as the aim is to provide an overall impression of the way events had moved by the time the Development Group withdrew from Brighton, they are not individually acknowledged.

The 'Residents' Rights' document is included at the end of this chapter. It enshrines a great deal of what the project was about, and therefore makes a fitting conclusion to this account of the events in Brighton.

SUMMARY OF DEVELOPMENTS final seminar, March 1979

Domiciliary care Perhaps the most considerable change in domiciliary care was in the way each service modified its view of its own role. Previously each service worked separately and considered itself to be the one which had priority cases. Now an awareness had grown up that domiciliary care could only satisfactorily be supplied by the united efforts of many different people, and the introduction of the interprofessional assessment form helped this process.

The administrative groundwork was the first thing to be tackled in bringing about changes. Home help time sheets were computerised and their clients indexed on the visual display unit. The relative duties of home helps and nurses were examined, and the needs for a Twilight Service and a Terminal Care Service were assessed.

Despite all the discussions it was still felt that the task in domiciliary care remained unclear, and uncertainty persisted about who should be carrying out the various duties involved. The home helps in particular considered that domiciliary care had not received enough priority and that it should now be the focus of future developments.

Fieldwork services There was some evidence that fieldwork with the elderly had become more 'respectable' at the final seminar. It seemed that the debate about the fieldworker's role with the elderly had been opened up. More broadly based strategies for helping clients were now being used and allocations to residential care had improved.

Despite these changes field social workers felt angry and depressed because they considered they had not been in a position to contribute much to the exercise, and that it had been a considerable disadvantage that the debate on the care of the elderly had been largely internal, rather than being conducted jointly with health service personnel, which would have been more appropriate. In addition a nagging feeling remained that there was both misuse of social workers and underuse of other potential sources of help for the elderly.

Day care Whilst there had been a lot of fundamental thinking on the subject of day care the definition of this service remained elusive. Some likened it to adult education and thought it should provide stimulation to growth and development, whereas others retained a more limited vision of what a day care service should provide. Whatever the purpose the overriding problem of providing sufficient transport to enable the centres to be used in a flexible manner was unresolved, and therefore they remained underused.

Special housing The housing department's inclusion in the multi-disciplinary assessment experiment led to substantial changes in their thinking about the provision of housing for elderly people, and a working party on sheltered housing was set up.

Residential care It was in the field of residential care that the most substantial evidence of change emerged. More than anything else there were marked changes in attitudes, and these affected both staff and residents. The whole climate of opinion altered in respect of such diverse subjects as taking risks and altering the manner in which residents' visitors were received. These changes have been epitomised by the establishment of the annual Residents' Conference. At these conferences residents were given an opportunity to become a group and to develop a voice of their own.

Administrative changes followed in the wake of these changes in attitude. Admissions were more carefully planned and co-ordinated, and potential residents positively encouraged to have contact with homes and staff before a decision about admission was made. Regular reviews were introduced in many homes with the residents taking part. Reviews were held within three months of admission and at least annually thereafter. More facilities for short term care and schemes whereby the elderly person spent one month at home and one month in care were established, and there was a gradual spread of mixed homes.

Training was thought to be a vital element in achieving change and, although progress was made in introducing training schemes for those working in residential care more extensive programmes were required, including an increase in resources of various kinds.

There were extensive discussions, but regrettably little progress, in respect of the number and role of the residential and day care officers. They were very thinly spread and their role was not clearly defined. It was always clear however that many new developments depended in great measure on the professional support and guidance that these officers could provide.

Residents' Rights

The following statement was issued by the Brighton Division as a result of work undertaken in the project:

What you have a right to expect if you live in one of the County Council's homes for elderly people

I. Basic Rights of Residents

1. The main concern of our homes will be the quality of life of their residents.

2. Residents have the right to personal independence, personal choice, and personal responsibility for their own actions.
3. Residents have the right to care for themselves as far as they are physically and mentally able, and willing, to do so.
4. Residents have the right to have their personal dignity respected by others in every way possible, and to be treated, whatever their disabilities or frailties, as individuals in their own right.
5. Residents have the right to personal privacy, for themselves, their belongings, and their affairs.
6. Residents have the right to take a full part in decisions about daily living arrangements, to be consulted about any changes which may be proposed, and to have a genuine say in social services policies.
7. Residents have the right to the same access to facilities and services in the surrounding community as any other citizen, including registration with the medical practitioner and dentist of their choice.
8. Residents have the right to be given every opportunity of mixing with other people in the community, whether by going out or by inviting other people in.
9. Residents have the right to have their cultural, religious, sexual and emotional needs accepted and respected as well as the whole range of other commonly accepted needs.
10. Residents have the right to expect management and staff to accept the degree of risk that is involved in these principles, and not to have their personal independence unnecessarily or unreasonably restricted for fear of such risk.

II. Some practical applications of these rights

1. Coming to live in a home You will be able to make an introductory visit to the home and see round it before coming to live in it, unless ill health or an emergency makes this impossible. Whenever possible a member of staff of the home will visit you in your own home, or if need be in hospital, to discuss the change in advance and answer questions, and so that you can get to know each other.

Social Services will give you the fullest possible information about life in the particular home in which you will live, and each home will produce an individual brochure describing its particular features.

2. Rules and routines Unnecessary rules and practices, such as getting people up too early or obliging them to go to bed before they want to, will be discontinued. Daily routines will be as flexible and natural as possible, and above all designed to meet the needs and comfort of residents rather than other considerations. The overall aim will be a relaxed and comfortable atmosphere, with plenty of activity going on for those who want it.

3. Visiting Visiting by relatives and friends is completely welcome, and no restrictions will be placed on this, unless of course you particularly request this. You will be able to see your visitors in complete privacy if you wish. Wherever possible there will be facilities for you to make tea or provide refreshments for your visitors.

4. Belongings So long as there is enough space available, you will be able to bring your own articles of furniture and personal belongings into the home. Cupboards or drawers will be provided for residents to lock away personal belongings if they so wish.

5. Sharing of Rooms Two or more people sometimes have to share a room because of the way the older homes are designed and the great demand for places. Sometimes however people share a room because they prefer to have companionship. We would like to make it unnecessary for anyone to share who doesn't want to, and in particular to do away with rooms having more than two beds. At present it is hard to achieve this because it would mean losing a lot of badly needed places, but we intend to do all we can to make things better.

6. Living in Small Groups In several of our homes experiments have been made, with the agreement of the residents concerned, in grouping small numbers of people together for daily living purposes, with their own shared sitting room and dining room facilities. We would propose to encourage such developments in homes where residents and staff wish it, provided that the premises can be made suitable.

7. Making Decisions and discussing Policies Residents will have a regular say in the everyday running of the home, whether by residents' meetings or representative committee. Opportunities will be given in these meetings for suggestions and complaints to be made.

A Divisional Residents' Consultative Committee will be established to meet regularly with the Divisional Director. The Committee will be composed of representatives from each of our homes and will have the right to discuss all matters of policy and practice affecting the interests of residents, and to be consulted on any proposed changes.

The Annual Conference of residents representing all homes which has been successfuly held for the past two years will be continued.

8. Complaints The brochure for each home will include an explanation of your right to have any complaints heard by the officer-in-charge, and if satisfaction is not obtained, by a more senior divisional officer. The brochure will inform you how formal complaints should be registered.

Residents will also be kept informed of the name and address of the local Member of Parliament and the County and District Councillors for the ward in which the home is situated, so that they may approach any of these directly if they should desire it.

9. Care Staff Officers-in-charge will expect care staff to spend a reasonable part of their working time in personal contact with residents. Pressure of domestic and practical tasks sometimes makes this difficult to achieve, but it is emphasised that social contact with residents is an important part of the everyday work of all care staff.

East Sussex County Council
Social Services Department
Brighton Division

Bibliography

*Annable W Activities for groups *Age Concern Today* (reprint) 1974

*Brooks B A street warden service for town or country *Social Work Service Magazine*, December 1974

*Brown D Resident participation *Residential Social Work*. Vol 16 No 4. P 95 1976

*Brown L When the residents make the rules *Community Care* 5.5.76. pp 16/17

Bromley G Interaction between field and residential social workers *British Journal of Social Work* Autumn 1977

Consumer's Viewpoint In residence *Social Work Today* Vol 9. No 9. 25.10.99. p 19

DHSS Residential homes for the elderly: arrangements for health care DHSS 1977

Eastman M Medical noose that strangles the social work function *Health & Social Service Journal* 29.7.77 pp 1108/9

East Sussex Area Health Authority, Brighton Health District Care of the dying patient and the family February 1976

East Sussex Social Services Department Residential work in social work. Key Issue 1. The Elderly 27.7.76

*Gray M Will old people's homes be swamped by the confused elderly? *Residential Social Work*. Vol 16 No 10 pp 265/7 1976

*Hughes M E Home helps – five years on *Health & Social Service Journal* 17.4.76

*Knight L Fostering. Not just kids' stuff *Community Care* 11.2.76 pp 14/16

*Lansley J Caring for the old. A community approach *Social Work Today* pp 21/25

*Mandelstam D A common complaint *New Society* 29.5.75 pp 537/8

*Marks J Home helps under pressure *Health & Social Service Journal* 15.5.76 pp 894/5

Marsden N & Gupton H Interesting the old *Community Care* 16.11.77. pp 26/28

*MIND How to start a group home *Residential Social Work*. Vol 15 No 5 pp 138/140 1975

Newsletter Thoughts on institutional care *Demonstration Centres in Rehabilitation* No 10. Oct 1977

*Orriss H D A home with a difference *Health & Social Service Journal* 17.1.76. p 119

*Plank D Caring for the elderly: report of a study of various means of caring for dependent elderly people in 8 London Boroughs GLC: Director General's Policy Studies and Intelligence Board 1977

PSSC Residential care reviewed 1977

Daily living: questions for staff 1977

Rudd T W Being human in homes Public Health Vol 87 Nos 1/2 pp 5/8 1972

Simson M Freedom in the home *Community Care* 15.6.77 p 27

Struthers T Old – but they keep a purpose in life *British Journal of Occupational Therapy*. Vol 39, no 2, 1976

Thomas N, Gough J & Spencely H An evaluation of the group unit design for old people's homes Wyvern Design Group Social Services Unit University of Birmingham

Whitton J How to quench the last flames of independence in old age *Health & Social Service Journal* 3.6.77 pp 894/5

Whitton J Conspiracy against a truly caring system for the elderly *Health & Social Service Journal* 17.12.76 pp 2238/9

*These articles were used in preliminary discussions with staff of residential homes.

Development group reports, publications & films

Title	Year	Publisher
Care & Treatment in a Planned Environment	1970	HMSO
Community Homes – Design Guide	1971	HMSO
Reading Extracts and Guide to Further Reading for Seminar on Violence	1971	
Community Development Project and the Social Work Service – Sunningdale	1971	
From Approved School to Community Home – St Gilbert's	1971	
St Gilbert's – Follow up	1977	
Towards a Community Based Service – Cheltenham	1972	
Intermediate Treatment Project	1973	HMSO
From Approved School to Community Home – Eastmore House (1)	1973	
From Approved School to Community Home – Eastmore House (2) – Follow up	1975	
A Community Home Growing Up – St Christopher's	1979	
A Lifestyle for the Elderly – Craven House	1976	HMSO
Turner's Court – What Next? (1)	1974	
Turner's Court – What Next? (2) Report of the Working Party	1975	
Approved School to Community Home – St Vincent's (1) St Vincent's Community Home – Report of the Working Party (2) Approved School to Community Home – St Vincent's Day Conference (3)	1977	HMSO
Approved School to Community Home – Risley Hall (1)	1974	
Developments at Risley Hall Community Home – Day Conference and Working Party Report (2)	1976	
Community Work in a Central and Local Government Context – Blackpool	1975	
Intermediate Treatment – Birmingham Conference	1976	HMSO
Report on a Seminar on Community Homes at Digby Hall – Derbyshire and Lincolnshire	1975	
Decisions and Resources – Isle of Wight	1976	HMSO

Residential Child Care Policy in Kent (Northdowns)	1975	
Hostels for Young People – Hostels Project	1975	HMSO
Violence	1976	HMSO
Community Home Exercise at Carlton – Carlton Report	1976	
Carlton Follow Up	1978	
Working Together for Children and Their Families Vols 1 and 2	1977	HMSO
Aspects of Supervision and Intermediate Treatment	1977	
Intermediate Treatment – Planning for Action	1977	
Intermediate Treatment – 28 Choices	1977	
Records in Social Services Departments	1978	HMSO
Management of Community Homes with Education on the Premises	1978	
Supervision & Intermediate Treatment – A Seminar at Scarborough 1976	1978	
'IT in Action' – Film	1978	
'Seven Young People in Care' – Video – for professional use only	1980	
'Seven Young People Talking with an Audience' – Video – for professional use only	1980	

Copies available from Development Group: Tel. No 01 407 5522 Ext. 7507

Printed in England for Her Majesty's Stationery Office by Hobbs the Printers of Southampton
(2100) Dd0698219 K20 12/80 G327